Perry

A Transformed Transsexual

— A LIFE-LONG SEARCH FOR IDENTITY —

— WRITTEN BY THE MAN WHO LIVED THE STRUGGLE —

PERRY DESMOND

PERRY - A TRANSFORMED TRANSSEXUAL

by Perry Desmond

ISBN 13: 979-8-9877431-2-6

Original Copyright © 1978,
Metamorphosis Books
Ironton, Missouri

Current Third Edition Copyright © 2023

Published for the Author by

Metamorphosis Publishing
P.O. Box 367
Ironton, MO 63650

Perry - is the story of one man's quest for identity.

We knew him personally. There was never a more gentle or loving man. He was a good friend, effervescently joyful, and always exuberant in his love for others.

Sadly, Perry is no longer with us. He passed away on June 26, 1984, his death the result of a stroke. His book was a labor of love written from his heart, in an effort to reach out to the weary and troubled souls who find themselves in situations similar to his.

Perry wanted his story to remain in print as an encouragement to others. Without hesitation or any attempt to gloss over his past, he recorded his own firsthand experiences.

We have undertaken the reprinting of his book according to his request, knowing that there are many people whom he would have helped had he remained on earth. Part of the proceeds for this book will go to help inner-city/underprivileged children go to camp for free.

The pages of this book express his compassion for, and understanding of, those who feel trapped or tormented by a similar struggle for self-identity. This is a story that must continue to be retold.

That was Perry's wish, and we honor our friends wish.

The Publishers
October, 2023

Perry Desmond 1973 - After Massive Doses of Female Hormones, Plastic Surgery, Silicone Injections and Being Castrated . . .

CONTENTS

PERRY'S
DEDICATION:

This book is for
Mother
who never stopped loving me;
for Janice and for Miriam

**Perry Desmond as the
"Quiz Kid"**

**Perry Desmond as
"Buster Brown"**

A BIRTHDAY GIFT

Today is my birthday. I'm forty-one. For the first thirty-seven years of my life I thought God had made a mistake. He must have been up in heaven playing tiddly winks or something when I was born. He should have pressed the "girl" button, but he pressed the one for boys instead! I wanted desperately to be a woman, and to have money, fame, and pleasure. All of that became a reality, but it wasn't enough. Oscar Wilde, the famed homosexual author of the Victorian era, once said, "In this world there are only two tragedies. One is not getting what one wants, and the other is getting it." I got what I wanted only to find that Wilde was right—something was missing.

On February 9, 1974, at 5:00 p. m. , I found what I'd been looking for all my life. This is the story of my quest. It is a shocking, sordid story. I've tried not to leave anything out.

It is my hope that the mistakes I made will help others find a shorter route to fulfillment and happiness.

This book, then, is my birthday gift to you.

Perry Desmond
Los Angeles
August 15, 1977

Perry at Age 15

Perry at Age 8

Above: Perry at The French Box Revue

Below: Perry (in the center) with Friends

1

I'm Buster Brown!

Most male transsexuals say that they feel like a woman trapped in a man's body. I felt the same way. In fact, I convinced myself that I *was* a woman, even though others didn't seem to realize it.

My story could have a happy beginning, on the stage, in one of Chicago's biggest nightclubs, as I rubbed elbows with Sammy Davis, Jr. , Della Reese, Dinah Washington, and other top celebrities.

It could have a sad beginning, when I was twenty-one, working as a male prostitute in a gay bar in New Orleans, consuming a fifth of brandy a day, taking "speed" to stay awake and barbiturates to fall asleep.

Or, it could have a traumatic beginning, as I looked into the toilet, saw it filled with bright red blood, and hobbled back to bed, wondering why I had mutilated my body.

But it should begin where it really started—in a small Louisiana town, on August 15, 1936, when I was born.

MOMMA'S LITTLE SISSY

My father was a pilot on a Mississippi river boat. He drank a lot. Maybe he was lonely, being away from home so much. I was always afraid of him. He would come home late at night, yelling, breaking things, Mother crying.

He used to drink up his whole paycheck at the bar and come home with a sack of fried fish or something for Mother to eat. One night she mashed the whole mess, fish, catsup, and all, in his face.

My early years were filled with many such traumatic scenes. Being the first child I had no one to turn to — so I began to build a fantasy world all my own. It was quiet and pleasant in "my" world. Everyone was happy there. I would go to my room and think about the beautiful starlets in the movies Mother took me to see on weekends.

That's when I first started dreaming about being a woman. Betty Grable, Alice Faye, June Haver, Jane Russell—they were my idols. I fantasized myself in their roles. This was my very private, "movie set," dream world. I escaped into it more and more as life grew increasingly difficult. I always felt out of place, never secure. I wanted to be a girl, but I was a boy.

Mother always worked. I used to go to her room, when she was away, and put on her dresses. I'd sit in front of the mirror, put on her earrings, lipstick, perfume, and rouge. I enjoyed posing there, pretending to be someone else—a Hollywood movie star—anyone . . . but *me!*

One day Mother came home early. She burst into the room and caught me in front of the mirror. I was so panic stricken I couldn't speak.

"Don't *ever* let me catch you doing this again!" she screamed.

She whipped me, harder, and harder, and harder, screaming, "You're a boy! You're a boy! You're a boy!"

She ripped the earrings off and threw them on the dressing table. I ran from the house crying.

AUNT EDNA

We lived in my grandmother's large, pre-Civil war house. Grandma, two of my uncles, Mother, Father, and my great aunt, Edna. Aunt Edna didn't agree with Mother the day I got whipped.

I went to her for consolation, snuggling against her breast.

"It's all right, Perry," she said gently. "You look nice dressed up that way. This will be our secret. You can come to my room and dress up whenever you want."

Looking back, I think I can understand why she spoiled me that way. She was a spinster. I can see her adjusting her wire-rimmed glasses with fingers beginning to gnarl with arthritis. Above her square, firm jaw, looking down through the bifocals at her sewing, her eyes were sad, always wistfully sad.

Rumor had it that years before she had been in love, but her sister stole the man's heart instead. He married my grandmother. They said it was a shock Edna never got over. She never dated again, but threw herself into her work as a seamstress for the wealthier people in town.

Her specialty was wedding dresses. Each beautiful gown must have reminded her that she would never wear one. She pinned news clippings of her wedding gowns, from the society pages, on the wall behind her sewing machine. My earliest recollections of her are working, bent over her sewing or cooking at the stove—always at work.

I was very special to her. Maybe I filled some of the emptiness. Early each morning she would bring me a cup of coffee. In the South, children drink coffee. They give you your "sip" every morning. Most children go to the kitchen for it. Aunt Edna brought mine to my bed.

She was a devout Catholic. She went to Mass several times each week. I remember her telling me, "Perry, don't worry.

Jesus knows your problems. He understands."

Each day when I came home from school she would fix me some sweets. Then I'd sneak in and put on a dress. I lived completely in a world of fantasy, women, and illusion.

The town we lived in began to seem drab and ugly. I started hating it there. I dreamed of the stage, Broadway, fun, music, and excitement. And in my dreams I always saw myself as a beautiful woman. Aunt Edna seemed to understand my discontent.

Mother was overprotective. She even let me have a girl's bicycle. I insisted on girl's toys, and Mom went along with it. She was upset with me for wearing girl's clothes but didn't seem to mind buying me feminine toys. It's hard to understand why, but that's the way it was. While other boys got footballs for Christmas, I got dolls and tea-sets.

My family was always interested in the theater. Several of them skirted the edges of show business, doing various jobs in the amateurish productions of a dying vaudeville tradition. One of my relatives designed sets. Another took part in a theater guild. I remember them doing the Andrews Sisters in drag. My uncle was Maxine. He seemed wonderful in the part. Watching him dance and sing, I was filled with admiration and envy.

BUSTER BROWN

My uncle got me a part in a production of "Carmen." I played a slave boy, and got to sing a few lines. My fantasies were fulfilled! It thrilled me to the marrow.

Someone from the leading department store in Baton Rouge told my mother they had seen me in the play and wanted me to be "Buster Brown" in a back-to-school shoe advertisement campaign. She agreed and I was off to the "big city."

Aunt Edna made the costume. It was cute, with ruffles, and I wore a blonde wig. Looking in the mirror, I felt an almost overpowering sense of freedom. At last—I was someone else! But I had to wipe off the makeup at the end of each day, take off the wig, put away the costume, and be me—a plain-looking little boy. My heart sank every evening as I traveled home.

One thought would cheer me—tomorrow I'd do it all again. The woman at the cosmetic counter would put a little makeup on my face, and some rouge on my cheeks. The blond wig would cover my own straight hair, and I would be "someone else" again. I would pass out comic books to all the kids who came to the shoe department.

"Where's your dog, Ty?" they would ask.

"I had to leave him home today."

My fantasy world would be a reality again!

WHY CAN'T PERRY PLAY?

"You're too big to do this anymore," the shoe department manager said one day.

"What do you mean?"

"Just what I said. Buster Brown is a little boy, and you're just getting too big. I'm sorry, Perry."

I was heartbroken!

I was afraid to play with boys. I went to a Catholic school, and the nuns seemed to understand my fears. They let me play with the girls. In fact, I played on the girls' softball team as a shortstop.

When tournament time came, however, it was a different story. Our coach, Sister Cecelia, called me over to the side of the field. She smiled a little nervously.

"Perry, you… you… just *can't* play in this tournament. I know how much it means to you, but . . . well, you just can't, that's all."

"Why not, Sister Cecelia?"

"You're . . . you're just not a girl, Perry."

"But you let me play for a *whole* year!"

"I know, but this is the tournament. You just can't play. You're a boy."

A large group of the boys had gathered around Sister Cecelia and I. They had always called me "sissy" and "Momma's boy," but, as they listened to her tell me I couldn't play on the girls' team, I heard them begin taunting me with a new epithet.

"Queer! Queer! Queer! Perry is a queer! Perry is a queer!"

I heard them chanting, louder, louder, louder! Tears streamed down my face as I ran from the field, down the street, into the arms of Aunt Edna.

"It's all right, Perry. It's all right," she said reassuringly. Later I went up to Mother's room and put on a dress. It was easier this way—in my "own" world.

THE ALTAR BOY

St. Luke's Church was a huge Gothic building. You had to pass my school next to it as you entered. Uncle Berk sang solos and the whole family attended Mass there every Sunday.

One of the sisters at our school told Father Roseland that I would make a good altar boy. Soon I was assisting him and his associate, Father Kershner. They gave me a long, flowing black robe and a white smock trimmed with lace.

I loved ringing the chimes during the consecration of the Host. But I was fearful at the consecration of the wine. Father Kershner used to push the chalice up as I tried to pour the wine. Only later did I realize that he didn't want me to pour in very much. I just didn't know what he wanted at the time.

My favorite part of the Mass was holding the paten under the chin of the communicants while the priest placed the Host in their tongues. As I looked into the open mouths of my family, friends, and especially the boys who teased me, I thought of how hypocritical they all were, and how funny Uncle Berk looked with his mouth gaping that way. It wasn't until years later that I realized my own hypocrisy.

Part of the responsibility I had as an altar boy was to swing the incense burner back and forth, walking down the aisle toward the coffin during funerals in the church.

I hated these funerals, the wailing, the darkness, and the fear. I tried to focus my mind on Ginger Rogers or Betty Grable singing a happy song, rather than on the dreary funeral dirge, filtering down from the organ through the gloomy recesses of the church. I was never very successful in these fantasies, however. I tried to avoid assisting at funerals whenever possible. I absolutely refused to serve when Uncle Berk died.

During this time I became very fearful of death and of being alone. Whenever I would open a door to a dark room, a horror would come over me, as though something fearful and mysterious were about to jump out at me. This dread haunted me for *years*.

THE BIG COP

As a little boy, the other boys had tolerated me. But now I was approaching adolescence, and the line of distinction between me and the others was becoming increasingly sharp. They didn't want me around, and they made it clear. They called me ugly names and told dirty stories about me. I was the butt of all their jokes.

There were a few girls I could play with, but, more and more, I played alone, by myself, with my movie idols.

Each day, on my solitary walk home from school, I saw a big policeman who stood on the corner directing traffic. He would stop the cars while I crossed the street.

He was over six feet tall, blond, with wavy hair, and penetrating blue eyes. He was so big and masculine. He fascinated me. He was strong and . . . beautiful.

I didn't want him to catch me looking at him too much, so I started sneaking around some buildings, standing there in the shadows, watching him direct traffic. Then I would go to the corner, stop, and pretend to tie my shoe, so I could look at him close out of the corner of my eye. Sometimes I'd walk around the block four or five times, just to get another look at him.

Then one afternoon *he* wasn't there. I was disappointed, and I went into an ice cream parlor to buy a cone. I took the ice cream and rushed out the door. He was coming in at the same moment: I ran right into him, smashing the ice cream into my face. Wiping my eyes with my hands, I looked up—right into those penetrating eyes! He smiled.

"Hey, what's the rush, little fellow?"

He helped me wipe the mess off my clothes and led me back into the store. He put his arm around my shoulder and ordered me another cone. Shivers ran down my spine.

I hardly thought about the ice cream as I stumbled home. A wave of warmth enveloped me; the thought of him filled my mind.

"I guess I *am* a queer," I thought. "I wish I were a woman. It would be so much simpler."

RAH! RAH! RAH!

They were teasing me too much at the Catholic school, so I switched to the public school. It didn't work though. Four other boys from St. Luke's switched schools, too—and brought the rumors about me with them.

I couldn't face people now. I couldn't stand the insults and name calling.

Then one day in the gym, the entire student body gathered to elect cheer leaders for the year. The election was nearly over. About twenty students had tried out. Suddenly somebody yelled:

"We want Perry!"

A cheer went up, and they began to chant:

"We want Perry!"

"We want Perry!"

My face flushed with embarrassment. I wanted to run. Someone grabbed my arm and pulled me down from the stands onto the basketball floor.

"Here's Perry!" he yelled.

A cheer went up.

Then suddenly, I wasn't afraid.

The old "Buster Brown" feeling came over me in a wave.

"O. K. , everybody let's do this . . ." I shouted. I led them in a rousing cheer, ending with handsprings, a back-bend, a cartwheel, and the splits. The crowd literally went wild.

I was elected as one of the six cheerleaders, four girls and two boys. I ran home to Aunt Edna.

"I'm a cheerleader! They elected me today!" I danced around her chair.

"Wonderful, dear," she said, reaching out to take my hand. "I'll make your uniform."

It was a beautiful costume, green satin, with gold trim and a sash. Aunt Edna made it more feminine than the other boy's. The sleeves were billowy, a little like a woman's blouse. I bought two pairs of pants. They were so tight I could hardly breathe.

The team marched onto the football field that first night.

We ran out behind them. The crowd cheered wildly. I felt like I'd arrived. I was second from the left.

It seemed as though all eyes were on me as we led the first cheer:

> **"Rickety, Rackety, Rust.**
>
> **We're not allowed to cuss!**
>
> **But yammit to yell,**
>
> **We're gonna yell**
>
> **For our home team or bust!**
>
> **Yeaaah!"**

The second game was in another town. The girls wore makeup. Why couldn't I? It was far away from everybody I knew. We would be way out on the field. Nobody would know. My heart beat fast as I thought about wearing makeup with my bright green uniform.

It was dark when we got on the bus. Nobody noticed that I had on pancake base and rouge. Soon we were driving off into the night. There were no comments, but this was a big step for me—the first time I ever wore makeup in public.

After that I always wore it to the games. One night, as I was getting ready, Mother caught me. She was a little upset. "What are you putting that on for?"

"We're taking pictures tonight," I lied.

Coach Koenig noticed the makeup, too. He looked at me with a disapproving scowl as I walked past him toward the field.

He didn't say a word, but I could feel the glare of his eyes, burning into the back of my head as I rushed away.

He always avoided me, but now and then I'd look up and catch him staring at me. He'd turn quickly to avoid my gaze, a dark shadow coming over his eyes, one corner of his mouth pulled down in heavy anger.

THE BOXING MATCH

But I couldn't avoid Coach Koenig. He taught my chemistry class, as well as gym. All the football players took his class. They had it easy. He joked and horsed around with them in the lab. And they all made good grades.

I was pretty smart, and I tried really hard. On the final exam my pencil broke. I turned to the girl behind me, and whispered, asking her if she had an extra one.

Suddenly I felt a hand grasp my shoulder. It was Coach Koenig.

"Desmond, come with me," he growled.

We went outside. I was trembling.

"What is it?" I asked.

"Why are you asking Nancy the answers?"

"I wasn't. I was only asking her for a pencil."

"That's a pretty good story! Almost as pretty as your face?" he snarled. "Get back in there, and no more talking!" I got a very low grade in the class.

Coach Koenig taught gym too, and I dreaded it. I was afraid to take off my pants, so I wore my gym shorts under them when I went to school each day. The shower room was a fearful place for me. The boys mocked and teased me there. It was easier to go into the locker room and pull on my clothes there after gym class, and not take a shower.

One day the coach caught me doing this. He started yelling, "Who do you think you are! I've had just about enough of you! Makeup, sissy-acting, cheating on tests! Desmond, I'm going to fix you good! You're going to do what all the other boys do—starting tomorrow. You're going to work, Desmond. You're going to *work*—do you hear?" He waved his fist in front of my face. "Basketball, football, and boxing—starting *tomorrow*! That'll make a man of you!" He was white with rage.

The nightmare started as scheduled. Each day I stumbled into the gym to begin "training" for my "big fight." I punched lamely at the bag a few times. I felt like a fish out of water. I didn't belong there.

As I punched at the bag, a big boy shoved me in the back.

"Hey, Perry-Fairy! How's the boxer? You gonna wear lipstick in the ring?"

The "big" day was drawing near, and, when I thought of it, my heart beat fast with fear. How could *I* be a boxer? How would I feel? What would I do? I could hardly sleep the night before the match.

That morning it was hard to eat breakfast.

"If only this was all a dream," I kept thinking. "Maybe if I phone the school and tell them I'm sick. . . " But there was no way out.

The sky had a pale, sickly gray cast, and the wind was chilling as I stumbled out the door and headed toward school.

The morning went by fast, like a bad dream. Coach Koenig confronted me in the gym.

"Desmond, I want you here on time tonight. The whole school will be here. Don't be late if you know what's good for you."

Fear welled up inside me.

That night I was the first one there. I sat in the gym room, trembling like a caged animal. I could hear the students filling the gymnasium. Then Coach Koenig came into the locker room.

"Is that you, Desmond?" he shouted, as I tried to hide in the shadows.

"Yes," I replied weakly.

"Well, get out there. They're waiting to see you fight!"

I made my way numbly out of the locker room, down the gray hall, through a door, into the crowded, sweaty-smelling gymnasium.

It seemed like every eye there turned to stare at me. Then the chanting started.

"Perry is a fairy! Perry is a fairy!" It was only a few of the boys who taunted me every day, and they were soon diverted from their fun as the first match began.

I was to fight in the second match. My skin felt blue with anxiety by this time. Sweat poured from my face and hands.

The voice of the announcer snapped through the microphone, "Eddie Villarreal will now fight Perry Desmond."

"Oh God, this is it," I thought.

I can't even remember stumbling into the ring. I do recall getting caught in the ropes though. I got all tangled up. Then someone pulled my arm and I was in the ring. There was no place to run!

Before I could even look around something smashed into the side of my head. I fell heavily to the canvas. "Get up, you sissy," somebody yelled.

I did. Eddie slugged me again, and again, and again. Blood rushed from my nose.

Through the blood and sweat falling in my eyes, I looked out across the ropes. They were *all* there—the whole student body! Eddie slugged me in the face again. I fell a second time.

The ceiling twirled madly above me as I lay there. They were *really* yelling now.

"Perry is a fairy!"

"Perry is a fairy!"

"Perry is a fairy!"

"Isn't *she* cute!"

"Look, she's fighting!"

"Perry is a fairy!"

"Perry is a fairy!"

"Perry is a fairy!"

The whole room was whirling. Blood flowed down my chin as I crawled through the ropes, ran up the aisle, and out into the night. Down the sidewalk, onto the street, faster and harder, I ran. My clothes were forgotten in the locker room.

The door of our house slammed behind me. I rushed into my room and fell sobbing on my bed.

"Oh, God! Where can I go? Who can help me? I'm *really* supposed to be a girl, that's what's wrong. I was cheated . . . by somebody! I'm a girl trapped in a boy's body! Oh God! Who can help me? No one! No one! No one!"

2

THE BUCKET OF BLOOD

The town I was born in was near New Orleans, so I went with my family to the Mardi Gras every year. During the Mardi Gras season we also had a children's carnival in our little town. Everyone got into costume and marched in the carnival parade which circled back and forth through the business section. I always pleaded with Mother to let me dress like a woman. But she refused, so I had to be a clown, or an Indian, or a cowboy (which I hated most).

I was especially excited about it this year. Mother was at work, so I ran home, put on a skirt and blouse, a bandanna over my head, gold hoop earrings, lipstick, and a small mask over my eyes. I was a gypsy girl!

I marched all over town in the parade, and no one knew who I was. I'd pulled it off! Everyone thought I was a girl. I felt *very* confident behind my disguise. I felt that this was the "real" me.

The parade passed a doctor's office. He and his nurse were standing outside watching. I flounced up to him, pulled up my skirt, and asked, "What do you prescribe, Doctor?" Everyone laughed.

I felt a strange power flowing inside me. It seemed to take over my whole being. This surge of power came over me in a similar way many times in the years to follow, *each time* I put on women's clothing. It was like the difference between Clark Kent and Superman—or Wonder Woman! I was no longer shy and afraid when I dressed in drag. I was arrogant, proud, and defiant!

JOLLY'S PLACE

In our little town, in the early fifties, the kids had nothing better to do on Saturdays than go to the movies—all day!

Roy Rogers, Flash Gordon, Superman, and cartoons—dozens of them.

And, on top of all that, a feature-length movie like "The Outlaw," with Jane Russell, "Blood Alley," with John Wayne, "Son of Paleface," with Bob Hope, "The Dolly Sisters," with Betty Grable and June Haver, and my favorite, "Look for the Silver Lining," with June Haver. Everybody at our high school went on Saturdays.

They were there that afternoon, all of my tormentors, as

the movie ended and the kids trickled out in little groups into the muggy, late afternoon air. I was alone, as usual. Turning the corner by the theater, I saw them, leaning loosely against the building. I braced myself, waiting for the insults to begin. But they didn't come this time.

"Hey, Perry, want to go with us to Jolly's?" one of them called.

"Yeah, come on, we'll have a good time," another chimed in.

I knew who Jolly was. Phillippe Joludow was a landscaper who lived alone at the edge of town. They called him "Jolly," and there were lots of rumors about him, including one about the boys that came there in groups several evenings each week.

"O. K.," I replied haltingly. *I did* want them to like me, and they seemed pretty friendly; maybe things would change after all.

As we approached Jolly's house, all the rumors I'd heard flooded my mind. Then the ringleader spoke. Jack Thompson lived right down the street from us. He was *always* picking on me, worse than any of the others. He spoke up.

"You're going to like this, Perry!"

We made our way on through the gathering darkness. My tongue felt thick; perspiration dripped from my clammy palms. What would I do? How would I react to it—whatever "it" was? I knew it was dark and secret and wrong, and I knew the rumors. I wanted to run.

"Hurry, come in," Jolly said, holding the door open as all twelve of us scurried in, and he shut the door quickly behind us.

I looked at him closely in the bright light of the room. His clothing was dirty, not filthy, but dirty, from working in the soil all day. Light reflected from the front of his bald head. His eyes danced with unnatural excitement as they darted from boy to boy. He licked the corners of his mouth and turned to me.

"You're new, aren't you?" he whispered. "I don't remember you." The words slid like oil from his lips.

Jolly headed for the bedroom, turning back to us at the door. "Who's first?" he asked. Jack Thompson, the ring-leader, literally *ran* in behind him. The door slammed shut.

It was an old house. There was a long crack at the edge of the bedroom door. The other boys crowded in close to peek.

I took my turn. There was Jolly . . . doing the *very* thing to Jack that I'd been accused of!

My shirt was cold with sweat when we finally left.

JOLLY'S SUMMER REPLACEMENT

"Come on, kid, let's go to Jolly's," Jack said a few nights later, standing there at our front door.

I didn't really want to, but . . . Jack was smiling, and he had been much nicer to me the last few days.

"O. K., wait 'til I tell Aunt Edna I'm going out."

But Jolly wasn't home when we got there. "Nuts! I was ready for this," Jack snarled.

The two of us got back in the car. He kept talking as we drove along in the dark. Then he reached for my hand. We stopped under a tree, and he turned to me, "Perry, why don't you do what Jolly does. I won't tell anybody. I promise."

When I walked into class the next morning, a big, red faced boy with pimples grabbed my arm.

"How about a date tonight, Perry."

He grinned, showing large yellow teeth, rimmed with green plaque.

"Jack said you're good at it. Come on!"

It was like that all day. Jack had kept his promise in a way. He hadn't told anybody. He'd told *everybody!*

Jack grinned when he came to my door a couple of nights later. "You're not mad at me, Perry, are you?"

"Well, no . . . I guess not."

"Come on out then. I want to tell you something."

As soon as I stepped onto the porch, he grasped the front of my shirt.

"You're taking Jolly's place, ya hear?"

He followed me to my bedroom. It was like that all summer. During the last few weeks, he started bringing his friends too.

The first one he brought really shocked me. There he was, our star basketball player, sprawled out on my bed. His voice was different than at school.

"Come on, Perry," he coaxed.

I had an inner conflict. "I'm queer," I thought. Another thought followed quickly: "No, I'm not really queer. I'm just a woman—trapped in a man's *body*."

As I bent over the bed, I tried to imagine myself as a girl. That made it easier and more fun somehow.

By now I dreaded waking each morning. My reputation was ruined. I knew what the day had in store for me at school. I would wait for the last second, and leave just in time for class. That way I wouldn't have to walk through all the students gathered outside talking.

During recess, I would never go out of the building. Instead, I'd slip into the music room and play the piano, or go up to the study hall and leaf through a magazine. I was becoming more and more isolated, lonely, and introverted.

One thing I would *never* do was go in the boy's restroom. I had learned not to do that when I went in, one day, and found a group of boys there smoking. They began to laugh at me.

"Ha! Ha! Aren't you in the wrong bathroom, Perry? Shouldn't you be in the girl's? Are you squatting, Perry?"

I ran to a stall and locked the door, my heart pounding.

"Let's go in there and see what's between his legs!" they teased. I huddled there in fear until the bell rang and they left. I never went into the boy's restroom again. I'd rather have had my bladder burst!

ESCAPE

At last I graduated! Mother sent me off to LSU. I was free! At seventeen, I was one of the younger members of my freshman class. But I *still* couldn't escape the rumors. Some of the boys from high school followed me to LSU. Soon the whispers and snickers started all over again. I began to feel totally trapped. There seemed to be no way out, no way to fit in anywhere. I was alone, in a hostile, angry world full of people who were out to hurt me, ruin my reputation, or use me in some way.

Then it happened. For the first time in my life, I met another person like myself—someone who could be my friend.

Lee was a little guy, but strong and masculine. I met him in modern dance; he was one of the lead dancers. We started running around together right away. Soon he had introduced me to almost every gay person on campus.

This was in the fifties, and all of us were still "in the closet," but we had our own way of identifying each other secretly. Through the gays Lee introduced me to, I got a job as an usher in a movie theater in downtown Baton Rouge.

It no longer mattered that the "straight" people laughed and did mean things. I now had gay friends. For the very first time in my life, I had a group of people who accepted me as I was. At last—I was part of a group. I felt free from loneliness! I "came out" with a bang!

THE DEAN'S OFFICE

A friend pulled me to one side as I was going down the hall to class one morning.

"They caught Bill last night," he said in a hoarse whisper. "Somebody opened the door and caught him with Roy. You're in for it too, Perry. Don't ask me why, but you are. The Dean wants you in his office right away. You better get up there quick!"

I fidgeted and fussed around in the hall, trying to get up courage, then I braced myself and entered the office of Dean Philpott.

"Perry, sit down, will you?" the Dean said, a strained

smile revealing large, obviously false, white teeth. He brushed his hand nervously over the short, vaselined hair plastered in strands across the top of his balding head. I noticed the broken tooth of a comb pasted into the hair at the side of his head.

He paced the floor a few times, stopped and seemed to pull himself together. Then he spoke, "Can you tell me anything about homosexuality here on campus?"

"Not really," I replied, half-truthfully, because *I didn't* know all that much.

Then came his second question, "Are you homosexual?"

I felt trapped. Then, just as suddenly, I felt bold.

"Yes! Yes, I am!" I exclaimed, a little surprised at my own voice.

Dean Philpott's face turned as white as his false teeth.

"Well," he stammered, "you can either resign now, or . . . if you stay, you'll have to watch your step. We're going to have our eye on you."

"Is that all?"

"Yes, that's all," he said in a thin, strained voice.

I didn't finish the semester, though. Everything was coming apart. I had "found" the gay community. This was what I wanted, not school.

POPULAR AT LAST

As a seventeen-year-old "queen," I became extremely popular in the gay community of Baton Rouge. I was "fresh," "unused," and everybody wanted me. I was needed, sought out, "loved"— at last!

The house was gray, unpainted, crumbling, like something a Southern Dracula might live in. Moss hung from huge trees in the yard. The second and third stories had large picture windows, opening out onto rickety balconies.

It should have been a dreary place, but it wasn't. Lights beamed from every window as we pulled up in Lee's car in the early twilight. This was a gathering place for homosexuals in the area. My friend Lee and I went in.

They were drinking. Somebody shoved a glass at me. I took it, and stood there, a little stiffly, wondering what to do next. It was my first such party.

I noticed a man looking at me from across the room. He came over, and we started talking.

"Let's go get something to eat," he said after a few minutes. We did, and I went home with him. We spent the night together. When he phoned me a couple of days later, wanting me to come back, I did. In fact, I moved in with him. He was at least twenty years older than I was. Ralph was my first "sugar daddy."

One night Ralph said, "I'm going to show you something

you won't forget."

We got in his white Nash Rambler and drove off to New Orleans, 82 miles away. We got there at about 10:00 p. m., and he took me to the French Quarter.

"Here's the place," he said. We went around to the back and came in through a passageway leading through the kitchen of The Starlite Lounge.

"Perry, it's illegal for you to be here, so shut up and keep out of sight."

I was still only seventeen.

The place was really jumping. It took a few minutes for my eyes to adjust to the darkened room. Then I looked up. Down the long bar, men were dancing together to the rock-n-roll hit, "Earth Angel." The music throbbed as they danced.

I looked up at the man behind the bar. His hair was bleached white. He had on bright red lipstick. Ralph told me his name was Ricky.

This was in the fifties, and gay bars where dancing was allowed was unheard of. I was shocked down to my socks, but thrilled with the dark atmosphere, pulsing music, and all the men—the hustlers in leather jackets, the queens in makeup. From the far corner, half hidden in the darkness, I watched them.

"This is for me," I told Ralph. "Someday I'll work in a

place like this."

MOTHER RETURNS

Mother heard about Ralph and I living together. She showed up one morning, insisting that I leave Ralph and go back to LSU. She didn't know the real reason I had left, because I'd lied to her.

I told her I'd go back to college, but not to LSU. I suggested a small college in Lafayette, and she agreed. I was off to Southwestern Louisiana Institute.

Nobody knew me at SLI. I could do whatever I wanted. Now I *did* feel free! Bleaching my hair was the first step, then makeup, mascara, rouge, lipstick . . . every day! I wore outlandish clothing—everything!

I'd go into the bathroom and put on my makeup every morning. The country boys in my dorm were flabbergasted, to say the least! They started calling me Liberace. I was the talk of the campus.

The gay bar in town was called The Buckhorn. Homosexuals from the whole district came here to make pickups. I told jokes and did songs and dances, all to gain attention and approval.

One night, as I was coming out of the movies, I met a boy named Chuck. He was beautiful. As we walked back to school together, we were amazed to find that we lived in the same dorm. We hit it off right away.

"I thought you were a girl when I first saw you," he said. "But it doesn't matter."

He was a "straight" country boy, but he liked me.

We started walking to classes together. Then he began visiting me in my room. We didn't have sex or anything, but I fell deeply in love with him. Finally we started kissing. Someone saw us one night and reported it to the Dean. Chuck's parents were there when we were called to the Dean's office. They asked us if we'd really been kissing.

Chuck spoke up, "Yes, yes we were." A look of deep anger and resentment spread over his face.

His mother's face turned pale. His father stomped out of the room. Then he stomped back in, yelling, "This school is *full* of queers! We're taking you out of college! You're going in the Army immediately! No son of mine is going to be a faggot!"

The Dean turned to me and said, "As for *you*, you'll have to leave. Now!"

Thus ended my second try at college.

THE BUCKET OF BLOOD

Now I was eighteen. *No one* could tell *me* what to do! I took the money they refunded me from college and headed for New Orleans.

The French Quarter was wonderful. It thrilled me to walk down the narrow streets, looking at the ancient two- and three-story French-style buildings, laced with wrought iron balconies. Although the Quarter is only about eleven by thirteen blocks, it contains literally hundreds of bars, many of them gay hangouts. It's a mecca for homosexuals.

I went to work as a waiter at Rikki Page's Bucket of Blood, on Esplanade Avenue, a street famed for its "dueling oaks," a group of old trees under which many lost their lives dueling in the last century.

Across the street from The Bucket of Blood was the old New Orleans Mint, where they once made Confederate money. The atmosphere was indeed steeped in history.

The Bucket of Blood was steeped in sin! Everything was done in deep red, with gold trim. At the end of the bar there were tables with red chairs. Couches covered with red velvet lined the walls. It was a haven for prostitutes—male and female. A steady trickle of "Johns" came in and out.

I was allowed to wear face makeup and lipstick. It wasn't long before I was "turning tricks" for money with the men who came there, a trade I became very adept at—male prostitution— at age eighteen.

It was here I first learned about "B" drinking. Girls would sit at the bar all day and into the night, asking the men who came in to buy them a drink. The drinks were a dollar each.

The girl's got a kick-back of fifty-cents on each drink. I became a "B" drinker after work. Some girls would guzzle twenty-five to fifty drinks each night. This wasn't as hard as it sounds, because the drinks were phony. They substituted cold tea for whiskey in them. I made lots of money—but I sure learned to hate tea!

Older men kept asking me to move in with them. But I wanted my freedom. All of that changed when Jerry came along. He was a wealthy tailor from Mississippi. He worked in one of the top clothing shops in the Quarter.

I was tired of work. He offered me an apartment, clothes, spending money, and only occasional sex with him. I took him up on it and moved in.

I started wearing women's clothes every day now. My own hair was long, and a queen in the building would comb it and set it for me every day. When I went out to the store or something, I'd flit in and out of the gay bars. Sometimes I'd pick up a trick that way.

I would get the male hustlers to take me to the movies. We would hold hands, just like a boy and girl. I was having a ball!

One morning the fun ended abruptly. Mother was at the door when I opened it.

"Can I see Perry?" she asked.

"Mother, *I'm* Perry!"

"My God, I thought you were a woman!"

She came in and sat down with a look of shock and horror spreading over her face. Then she began to tell me what was happening back home.

"Perry, they're all talking."

"Who, Mother?"

"Everybody! They're saying terrible things about you."

"What things?"

"Well . . . all kinds of things. They even say you're an herm . . . hermaphrodite."

"A *what?*"

"An hermaphrodite. And that you've had a baby."

"Oh, God! It must be horrible for you."

"It is, Perry! They're saying *such* terrible things."

"What can I do?"

"Please come home. Please come and stop the rumors."

I did. . .

THE NAVY

I cut my hair, got a pair of leather boots, and—of all the crazy things—joined the Navy. They sent me to boot camp in San Diego, and then to the hospital corpsman's school in

Portsmouth, Virginia.

While on leave one spring, I started dating a high school friend. I wasn't sexually attracted to her, but I thought I could force myself to "make it." I was wrong. We were married in the Catholic Church one weekend, but the honeymoon was a disaster. To my great embarrassment, I discovered on my wedding night that it was impossible to force myself to be a "man."

The marriage lasted a short while. We then separated and were later divorced.

Life in the Navy became more and more intolerable. By now I was convinced completely that I should have been a woman… or, maybe, that I really *was* a woman, caught by some dreadful quirk of fate in a man's body. At least that's what I told the psychiatrist at the hospital in Pensacola, Florida.

"Doctor, I'm really a woman."

He looked up at me with wonder. I don't think he'd ever encountered a transsexual before.

"I'm not a man. I like men, and I intend to start living as a woman."

He bent over some papers and began writing. I was committed to the Naval hospital as a "sexual deviate." Within weeks I was discharged.

Perry in the Navy

3
COMPULSION

I had failed in college.

I had failed in my marriage.

I had failed in the Navy.

Now I was certain I couldn't make it in the "straight" world. Most men are just beginning life at twenty-one. I felt like mine was already over.

My parting shot at the Navy was to dress in full drag, plaster my face with makeup, and drive out the gate, my current lover at my side, honking wildly, and waving at the guards, who stood at stiff attention, their astonished gaze following us down the dusty road toward Baton Rouge.

My lover, Les, and I got an apartment in the city, and settled down to a "normal" life. Mother was glad to see me, but, although I took Les to her house for dinner one night, she didn't know we were living together. Neither did the officers of

Naval Intelligence, who were looking for Les. He was AWOL.

One night they came to Mother's house looking for him. They showed her his photo. She told them he had been there to dinner with me a few nights before, and gave them my address.

We were in bed when they knocked on the door. I answered it, and one of them shoved a badge in my face. They arrested Les for being AWOL and me for aiding him. At the police station, Les did a noble thing. He told them that I had picked him up hitch-hiking, that I didn't know he was ditching the service. They let me go. I waved to him as I walked free into the night. I've never seen him since.

CANDY LEE AND EDWARD G.

Without Les I was lonely. Baton Rouge seemed dull and lifeless. I took off for New Orleans.

I got a job as a waiter at Tony Bacino's famed gay bar, and was right back where I started.

The notorious Candy Lee was performing in the patio bar at the back of Bacino's. She was really something—talking filthy, showing pictures of herself with various movie stars, doing obscene gyrations, and making cracks at the people, many of them famous, who came to see her unusual act.

Candy took a liking to me. It wasn't long before she was

"fixing me up" with some of the rich old "Johns" who were friends of hers. I began giving them my telephone number.

Before long I was running a call service. I soon had too many to handle myself. I was spending the whole day turning tricks. Then I began giving some of the names to other boys. It just sort of evolved. I was head of a very profitable call boy ring. I got a percentage of each one's take.

Life at Bacino's was thrilling to me. I waited on top celebrities—Paul Newman, Joanne Woodward, Angela Lansbury, Raymond Burr, Edward G. Robinson, and others. I wasn't really satisfied with my life as a waiter, however. Show business called me like a siren on the rocks.

MY-O-MY

One night a friend told me they were looking for a female impersonator at the My-O-My Club. I went down to audition.

The club was built on a pier, out over the water of Lake Ponchatrain. You had to walk under a long candy-striped canopy out to the club's entrance. Bold red letters on the awning read:

CLUB MY-O-MY
WHERE BEAUTIFUL GIRLS
ARE REALLY BOYS

I stopped to read the sign, then looked out over the lake.

The lights of the building were dancing on the water. I turned and walked into the club.

On the walls in the lobby were huge blow-ups of some of the most famous female impersonators in America—Julian Eltinge, Titanic, Mario Costello, Leynon, T. C. Jones, and others. A thrill ran down my spine as I passed them and headed toward the dressing room.

"If only . . . no, I'll *never* make it big like them," I thought.

They showed me to a dressing table, and I sat down to put on my makeup. I must have really seemed nervous, because Leynon, one of the top stars there, came over to comfort me. In a heavy Spanish accent, he said, "My dear, you're very beautiful, but you can't go on stage with such *light* makeup. You'll fade out under the lights. Come over to my table and I'll fix you up." As I followed him over to his dressing table, I noticed the room for the first time. It was a mess! The makeup tables were shoddy. Beer and wine bottles, ash trays, makeup, costumes, and garbage were strewn everywhere.

Three smells mixed in the heavy atmosphere—the stench of dried sweat, stale alcohol, and heavy cigarette smoke. It was nearly unbearable. But I was so excited I hardly noticed. I was in heaven.

I sat down at Leynon's table. Without a word he started applying grease paint, eye-liner, mascara, rouge, and lipstick to my face. Then he took out one of his long, brown wigs and

**LEYNON- The Female Impersonator Who Helped
Perry Get Started In "Drag"**

put it on me. The wavy tresses hung down over my shoulders.

"There," he said, "How do you like that?"

I looked in the mirror. It was someone else! Not Perry, not Buster Brown, but a *beautiful* woman. Another thrill ran down my spine.

Then Leynon helped fix my costume. It was all done in silver: a brassiere with long tassels, bikini pants with a silver fringe, gloves that ran up to my elbows, with long fringe hanging from each arm, and a transparent umbrella with fringe that hung down to the ground around me as I held it. It was a striking costume—all bright silver, with the light filtering through the gauzy, clear streams of the parasol. Aunt Edna had spent weeks making it for me.

"Don't worry, Perry, you're a natural," Leynon whispered.

I was so very grateful for his help. It saddened me a few years later when I heard that he had been beaten to a pulp, his face an unrecognizable mass, a twelve-inch wooden stake driven up into his body. I couldn't go to the funeral, though, because it all happened in Mexico, and we didn't even hear about it until after he was buried.

He flashed a smile at me that night as I stepped toward the wings to go on. My heart beat fast as I stood there in the darkness waiting. I glanced down at the music sheets in my hand, "Harlem Nocturne," "Night Train," and "Avalon."

"O. K., sister, what's your name?" the MC growled behind

me.

"Why, uh, Perry Desmond," I replied.

"No, no! What's your *stage* name?"

"I don't have one," I said weakly.

"Well," he snorted, *"nobody* uses their real name. Make one up. Quick!"

I gulped and looked down at the sheet music in my hand. My eye fell on the title of the first piece.

"Uh . . . call me . . . call me Avalon," I stuttered. He pushed me onto the stage.

The music stopped and the MC grabbed the mike.

"Ladies and gentlemen, for the first time on any stage, anywhere—here's the sensational, the beautiful—Avalon!"

The music throbbed again, and I moved to the center of the stage. The lights blinded me. I was frozen with fear. The applause rose, then died down. Suddenly the old "Buster Brown" feeling welled up within me. I was on—and ready!

I paraded up and down the stage to the roll of the drum, twirling my transparent parasol. I could "feel" the approving eyes of the audience. Warmth rolled over my body in waves. I cocked my head back and strutted like a peacock. I was *somebody!* I had arrived!

The manager told me I was hired but I would have to wait a while before I could get into the show. I became a waiter.

I tried to put on a happy front, but I was still miserable inside. I would take speed to get going in the morning, drink almost a fifth of brandy a night, and then take downers to go to sleep. I could hardly stand going to bed with all those old men! Why couldn't I just wake up one morning and be a woman? Then some nice looking boy would fall in love with me and marry me! Love was what I craved, more than anything.

THE JEWEL BOX

The Jewel Box Review was the most fantastic drag show ever to hit the American stage. It featured twenty-five men and one girl (who impersonated a man). The Jewel Box originated in Miami Beach, played the better night clubs all over the country, and eventually went to Broadway.

Can you imagine my surprise when Danny Brown, the owner of the Jewel Box Review, came into the My-O-My and sat at a ringside table a few days later?

I only had on face makeup, as I waited on tables, when Danny came in.

"If only I were dancing, I might have a chance," I thought.

My mouth must have fallen wide open when they told me he wanted me to come to his table.

I could hardly breathe as I sat down. I wouldn't have been

more excited if it had been Sam Goldwyn or Florenz Ziegfeld! I looked at him closely. He was so impressive, wielding the power of life or death in this sector of the entertainment world. His hair done perfectly, he was tanned and looked much younger than he was. But it was his eyes that caught your attention. They had a curious glint, penetrating, as though he could see your innermost thoughts. He looked a little like John Barrymore.

"Sit down," he said. I obeyed, a little self consciously, wondering what he would say next. "How would you like to be in my show?"

What could I say? I was thunderstruck.

My head swirled; I felt like I was on a merry-go-round, and had just snatched the golden ring—for a free ride!

A PLACE I SHOULDN'T BE

I gave away everything that wouldn't fit in the big wardrobe trunk I bought at the Salvation Army store. Buzzing all over the Quarter, I bragged to everyone that I had made the "big time." Months later I discovered the real reason Danny Brown had picked me. It was my size, the same as the little queen who had left their show. They wouldn't have to remake his expensive sequined wardrobe. It was cheaper for them to train me to take his place. What a blow that was to my ego.

Kasee's Club was two stories high, had a wrap-around

balcony with tables on both floors for the diners, and a large stage. It was a posh supper club. My friend Troy and I entered as the middle production number was going on. We went upstairs to watch from the balcony. I had never seen such costumes, so much glamor and talent all heaped together on one stage in my life. It nearly took my breath away, like a Las Vegas revue, and they were all men in drag, with one girl dressed as a man. They were perfect.

The production number was followed by something I didn't even know existed, a male toe-dancer. Then the comedian Gita Gilmore, came flouncing onto the stage to do his impression of Sophie Tucker. In later years I shared a dressing room with Gita, watching this former great drink himself deeper and deeper into the special hell that alcoholics create for themselves.

But that would come in the future. This first night, he was fresh and sober. He belted out Sophie's great song, "Some of These Days:"

> Some of these days,
>   You're gonna miss me, honey!
> Some of these days,
>   You're goin' ta feel so sad!
> You'll miss my lovin'
> You'll miss my kissin'
> You'll miss your red hot mamma—

Some of these days!

And when I leave you,

I know it's goin' ta grieve you.

Some of these days.

The curtain rang down. The lights dimmed. The drum rolled. A voice came from off-stage. Pearl Bailey? No—it was Lynn Carter, the star of the show:

Won't you come home, Bill Bailey?

Won't you come home?

I've searched the whole night long.

I'll do the cookin' honey,

I'll pay the rent.

I know I've done you wrong.

Remember that rainy evening

You put me out,

With nothin' but a fine tooth comb?

I know I'm to blame;

Ain't that a shame?

Bill Bailey, won't you please come home?

He sang, talked, and looked exactly like Pearl Bailey, for over twenty minutes. The curtain came down to thunderous applause.

Then came the finale. The chorus line was all in pink. They had on huge hats with rhinestones and ostrich plumes. They moved with pin-point coordination, doing "lifts" and "spins."

Somehow, I couldn't picture myself on stage with them. I just wasn't good enough. This was a place I shouldn't be.

I wanted to run, swim, fly—anything—to get back to New Orleans!

After the show, the entire cast came upstairs to meet Troy and I. One of the chorus "girls" was an old friend of mine from the French Quarter. It made me less uneasy to see him.

"Do you know Troy, Perry?" someone asked.

"Yes," I replied, "we came up together from New Orleans."

Later that night Troy and I moved into the hotel where the cast was staying. Then we all went out drinking. I got drunk, a routine I followed throughout this phase of my life.

The next day we gathered at the theater for rehearsal. The choreographer called us and gave us our assignments. Troy was a show "girl" and I was placed with the chorus line. Hours of rehearsal began, fitting Troy and I into the perfect precision of the show. Although the other members of the cast must have had some resentment at taking all this time to fit us in, they never showed it. They were wonderful and very patient.

My past experience, as a dancer and cheerleader, came in

handy now. In the "can-can" number I had to do high kicks on the table top, handstands, and run across the stage, landing in a split. Buster Brown had nothing on me! It was grueling work, but I was in seventh heaven.

There's no way of telling how many production numbers I messed up in front of large crowds, but soon I was a seasoned performer, as confident as the rest, my ego and pride growing rapidly.

The show moved from Toledo to The Cat and Fiddle, in Cincinnati. Money was *rolling* in, not only from the show, but from the tricks I was turning on the side.

WASHINGTON

From Ohio, The Jewel Box Revue went to Washington, D. C. , to the plush Casino Royale. I was thrilled to be in the Capitol for the first time. It was even more thrilling to follow such stars as Sophie Tucker and Johnny Mathis on stage. We were there for months, playing to packed houses every night. Senators, diplomats, and congressmen were sprinkled through the audience many nights. Secret service men were everywhere on those occasions. Ike was in the White House, Nixon was arguing with Kruschev, the Washington gays were in the closet, and the Washington police kept a close watch on the antics of The Jewel Box Revue.

That Christmas I flew to New Orleans with my new wardrobe and my beautiful leopard coat (imitation). I hit all the old bars. People were stunned at my new image. I flashed photos of myself with top celebrities everywhere I went. I had a phony newspaper headline printed to show them, "LOCAL BOY MAKES GOOD AS GIRL." I used every second of my two weeks leave visiting and bragging on my career.

When I went home for Christmas dinner, I took off my makeup and dressed in men's clothing. Everybody was there, my whole family. Mother took me to the kitchen, whispering in my ear angrily, "Why are your eyebrows plucked and your nails and hair so long? What will people think?" Later at dinner, she told the family I was in the theater.

"You *know* how strange show people are," she said, as she passed the turkey.

My Dad was there, and he didn't buy her story. He looked at me from time to time with anger. He had never quite forgiven me for the time, years before, when he had been drinking in a bar where they were joking about the little "queer" who dressed like a woman. Two hours later he realized who they were talking about—me, his son!

It was very uncomfortable sitting there. My cousins stared at me as I choked down a piece of dry turkey. I couldn't wait to get back to "my" world.

It *is* the "Windy City." An icy gale cut through my coat as I stumbled up the hotel stairs, a suitcase in each hand. I checked into one of the "better" rooms.

"You're coming up in the world, Perry," I thought, plunking down my luggage and looking around at the expensive furnishings.

The rest of the cast was there already. I was late, so I rushed back onto the street, got a cab, and headed straight for rehearsal at Robert's Show Lounge.

Looking out the window of the taxi, I noticed the marquee of The Black Orchid, *the* club in Chicago. The words jumped out at me:

TONIGHT — SAMMY DAVIS, JR. — IN PERSON!

I looked through the opposite window. My heart leaped; there was a life-size picture of Della Reese in front of Mr. Kelly's. The street was lined with such clubs. Little did I realize then that I would return to several of them as a down-and-out stripper in the years to follow.

Chicago excited me. It was the city of gangsters, the Mafia, Al Capone, lights, excitement. The old song drifted through my mind:

Chicago, Chicago,
That toddlin' town;
Chicago, Chicago,
I'll show you around.

You'll love it!
Bet your bottom dollar,
You'll lose your blues in
Chicago, Chicago,
The town that Billy Sunday
Could not close down. . .

"Who was Billy Sunday, and why would he want to close Chicago down?" I thought fleetingly. Later I would find the answers to those and other questions, but tonight my thoughts were full of *me* and my future in "show business."

I was awed at the size of Robert's Show Lounge. It was almost a whole city block long. I rushed in, bumping into my old friend, Fran Novack.

"What are you doing here?" I gasped.

He flashed his beautiful smile, "Perry! I'm sure glad to see you!"

We sat down on a nearby couch as he continued talking.

"Well," he said, "I won the 'Miss Chicago Drag' contest the other day. Danny Brown just hired me to appear in the show."

I was overjoyed!

Fran later rose to the top of the drag world, only to be cut off in the middle of his career, dying suddenly one night from an overdose of drugs.

Fran and I walked into the lounge of the club and sat drinking coffee for a while, reminiscing about Bourbon Street. Then we went in for rehearsal.

We were putting in several new production numbers, revamping the entire show. Tony Midnight, the famed wardrobe designer, was there, taking fittings, and making sketches of our new costumes.

But my mind wasn't really on any of this; I was thinking about Chris. He was my lover in New Orleans. I had met him there while working at the My-O-My Club. He was a construction worker from Georgia. We had moved in together.

It was the first time I had really loved anyone . . except myself. When I'd left for this tour with the Jewel Box Revue, Chris was in jail for bad checks. Now he was out. I could hardly wait to see him.

I had a letter from him in my purse telling me that he needed plane fare to come to me. I wired the money to him on the spot. Tonight he was coming! My heart beat fast each time I thought of him that evening.

I kept watching the door, waiting for him to come in. He didn't show. Maybe he was going to surprise me by being at the hotel when I got home. I took off my dress and pulled on men's clothing, grabbed a cab, and headed toward the hotel. He wasn't there.

I phoned the airport. They told me he hadn't come on

the flight he had scheduled. A deep depression flooded me. I drank myself to sleep that night, and the next, and the next.

On the fourth morning, they buzzed me from the desk downstairs, asking if I would accept the charges for a collect call from New Orleans. Of course I would! It was Chris!

"I love you," he said softly.

"Where . . . what . . . What happened to you?"

"I'm sorry, honey. I met an old friend. Before I knew it, we spent all the money you sent on booze. Can you send some more? This time I promise I'll come. You don't know how hard it was to be locked up like an animal, and suddenly be set free. I just couldn't help myself. Please . . . I love you . . . please send me the money!"

I did, of course.

Later I found out his "old friend" was Linda, a Bourbon Street stripper—a *real* woman. That wasn't the last time I was to lose Chris to a woman. But I didn't know it then. I rushed him the money, waited breathlessly, and fell into his arms when he finally arrived.

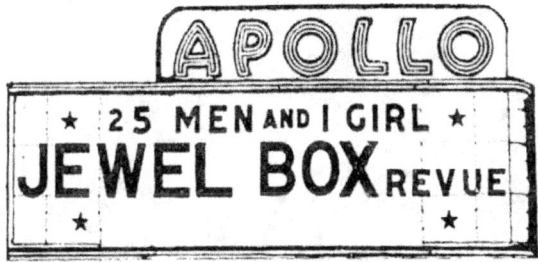

Perry and Chorus "Girls" in Can-Can Finale

DANNY BROWN
presents
His
JEWEL
BOX
REVUE

Candy Lee

Perry, Candy and Pauline

**Perry Desmond, Second from Left,
with Sammy Davis Jr. and the
Cast of the Show**

**Perry and Chorus Boy at the
Casino Royal in Washington, D.C.**

4

THE SOUTH'S MOST BEAUTIFUL BOY

Whiskey was a quarter a shot. I gulped another. My mind was foggy by now. Looking around the bar, I saw old men, crusty with filth, sitting on both sides of me.

Two or three hags with huge, sagging breasts cackled loudly. One of them was sucking the slack lips of the toothless drunk next to me, stopping now and then to down another shot.

Through the smokey haze of this skid row bar in Chicago's Old Town, the voice of the soloist rose above the subdued din of drunken voices:

> They're playing songs of love,
> but not for me.
> A lucky star's above,
> but not for me . . .

I turned to look out the window. A man was lying in the gutter outside, clutching a half-empty bottle of wine in his claw-like hand. "What am I doing here?" I thought suddenly. I got up to leave. The words of the song followed me out into the night:

> Although I can't dismiss
> the memory of your kiss,
> I know it's not for me.
> They're playing songs of love,
> but not for me . . .

Snow was falling as I stumbled back to the hotel.

Chris had left me for good.

The Jewel Box had a two-week lay off.

Christmas was coming.

I was alone.

There was nothing to eat in my room. I opened the window and took a gallon of muscatel wine from the snowy sill. As I poured a glass, I caught a reflection of myself in the mirror. What a sight I was! Dark circles rimmed my eyes, my cheeks were gaunt, my hair was matted.

Chris had gone suddenly one night while I was at work. He left a note, "Perry, I have V. D. The doctors told me today. I'm leaving. Sorry, Chris."

He took my money, savings and all. A clerk at the hotel told me he had been blowing it on girls while I was at work. I refused to believe him at first. Now I knew it was true. I was penniless and alone, without even my job to fill up the time.

Where had I gone wrong? I had given Chris everything. Was love only a word people mouthed? Where was love for me? Maybe I wasn't enough of a *woman* to keep him. I sat on the edge of the bed and cried.

LOOKING FOR LOVE

During the next few days I pulled myself together. Then the Jewel Box opened again, and I threw myself into the work. I was ready to go out and find someone to love.

One night I stepped into The Grill on Chicago's Near North Side. It was a nice, gay restaurant. There he was! I knew it as soon as I saw him. I smiled across the table. He was with a group, but he got up and came over.

"Can I join you?" he asked.

His name was Doug. He was clean-cut and very handsome.

That night he came home with me. He came back every night after that.

Life was starting to sparkle again. Then one morning Doug woke me early. I sensed something was wrong.

"Perry, I want to take you somewhere," he said.

We got in his car and drove out of the city to a suburban tract of homes. We stopped, got out, walked past tricycles, toys, a swing set, and into the house.

Doug went to the piano. "Look at this, Perry," he said, picking up a gold-framed picture. The photo showed him beside a woman and two smiling children.

"This is my family. This is my home. I'm married."

He spoke nervously, pushing the photo back on the piano. I followed him out to the car, not knowing what to say.

As we drove back to Chicago, he began opening up to me. He and his wife had been having sexual problems, stemming from his fears of being gay. It got so bad that his wife took the two children and went back to her mother. He had decided once and for all to find out if he was a homosexual. I had met him that night at The Grill. He had picked me because I looked so much like a woman that he felt it would be easier. He turned to me as we drove along, tears running down his face.

"Perry, I'm going to phone my wife and ask her to come home and forgive me. I love her. I'm not gay. I realize that now. I can't see you anymore . . . it's ruining my life." His words pierced my heart.

I stumbled up the stairs to my room. There was a telegram waiting for me:

PERRY—YOUR FATHER IS SERIOUSLY ILL IN OSCHNER'S HOSPITAL—PLEASE COME HOME IMMEDIATELY—WE NEED YOU—LOVE, MOTHER

"Oh," I thought, "what an awful time for this to happen!" My brother and sister were in high school. I felt sorry for them. Father had been drinking up what little money they had. I knew they needed me.

At the club that night, I went to Danny Brown and asked for a leave of absence.

"What! Are you insane!" he screamed. "We don't have anybody to replace you! Get on that stage!"

I did what he asked. It was the opening number, "Blue Mist." Everyone was dressed in blue-sequined costumes. I was on the front, in the chorus line. The chorus boys stepped in behind us and we fell in their arms. The music welled up.

Anger rose within me. I hated Danny Brown; I hated my father for being sick; I hated Doug; I hated this show; I hated everything!

I was overcome with rage. Right there, in front of a packed theater, I walked off the stage, stormed into my dressing room, ripped my dress off, and threw my wig on a chair. I was putting on my blue jeans when I heard Danny Brown's voice, "That's the trouble with you queens, you let a little applause go to your heads! You think you're indispensable! Well, you're not, Perry Desmond! Acts like yours are a dime a dozen!"

I pulled on my shirt, reached into my pocket; took out two nickels and dropped them in Danny's hand.

"Here's a dime. Go buy yourself a dozen," I said as I brushed past him out the door.

That night I boarded a train for home. It was a dreary trip.

YOU CAN'T GO HOME AGAIN

I went straight to the hospital. Dad was very ill with cirrhosis of the liver. Walking down the hall to his room, I thought of how little we had really communicated across the years. I hardly knew him.

Shock chilled my body as I looked at him there in the bed. What had once been a husky man was now so shriveled it was difficult to recognize him. He looked so weak and helpless lying there. I wondered how I could have ever been afraid of him.

A scowl swept over his face as he looked up into mine. I

knew what was going through his mind, "The morphodite is here." That's what he always called me, and I could read it in his thoughts now.

Mother sat in a chair by his bed. She looked so tired, haggard, and worn. A wave of sadness came over me. The poor thing was always there, always taking care of dying relatives.

We engaged in some rather stiff small talk for a while, then Mother and I went home.

They now lived in a small, wood frame house. Grandmother's big house was gone. Dad had wasted most of the family money. It was sad to see how far down they'd come.

I moved into the garage apartment behind Mother's house. Dad got out of the hospital and came home. But he wasn't the same; he was a beaten man, afraid to die. I avoided him as much as possible, especially now that I had a new lover living with me. Tom was an Italian from New Jersey. I met him in a New Orleans' bar. I was "in love" again!

I went to beauty school, and several months later I opened a salon in Baton Rouge. It did great. But new hostilities were growing between Mother and I over Tom, and the fact that I worked in drag across the river on weekends.

I tried to talk it out with her, but she couldn't understand why I was gay, or why I wanted to dress like a woman. I realize now that it was really impossible for her to understand these things, but it filled me with more frustration and anger at the time.

BACK IN DRAG AGAIN

I decided it was time to go back on the road. I had a list of clubs that had female impersonator shows. I called a few of them. One in Kansas City said for me to come right away. Tom and I loaded up our '57 Ford and headed for Kansas.

It was hell there. They wouldn't let me mix with the audience after the show, so I had to start hustling in the streets. Tom stayed holed up at home, getting stoned on drugs and watching TV. Sometimes I had to go out in snow ankle-deep to make extra money for his drug habit. But I enjoyed the suffering in some perverse way. It was like a movie—the lazy pimp and the abused prostitute!

We finally moved on to Chicago. I got a job in a strip joint on Rush Street. They let me turn tricks on the side. One night I rolled a rich John for everything he had, and Tom and I were off to New Jersey, where his parents lived.

We opened a beauty salon there, and were doing well. Then his family began to make trouble.

His mother started phoning him, telling him every dirty thing she could think of or make up about me. Soon her influence took its toll.

One day I was in the basement of her home doing something. Tom was in the kitchen having coffee with her. They were very wealthy and it was a huge house. I admired the expensive furnishings as I walked toward the kitchen. Stopping at the door for a moment to adjust my shirt, I heard her voice filtering through the door.

"Tom, you're getting too old. We've put you through school and helped you all we could. But you've got to think of your own future. You should get married and settle down. Instead, you're running around all over creation with that. . . that half-and-half!" She then offered him a car and money if he would leave me.

I choked back tears and pulled myself together. Entering the kitchen, I put on my best fake smile and said, "You know, I've decided to go to New York. The Jewel Box is playing on Broadway. Maybe Danny Brown will give me my old job again."

NEW YORK-NEW YORK

I took off for the Big Apple, but the Jewel Box wasn't there when I arrived. They were playing in Long Island. I got a job at a beauty salon on Central Park West and tried to forget about Tom. It wasn't easy.

Through the front window of the salon I had a good view of the busy street. I saw a number of celebrities pass by: Ethel Merman (her mother lived in the building where I worked), Robert Goulet, Carol Lawrence, and others. I longed for the stage again.

One day a customer told me she was interested in seeing

my publicity photos. "Hey, she exclaimed excitedly, "these are good. Let me take them to a friend of mine. He's a theatrical agent."

A few days later I got a phone call from Phil Franco, the agent. He wanted to see me. He said he could book me all over the country, that there was a big demand for acts like mine.

I rushed over to see him. His office was right on Broadway. It looked just like something out of a movie. The overly-made-up secretary greeted me with a brassy, adenoidal, "New Yorky" accent.

"What's your name," she yelled.

She pressed a button and Mr. Franco came out. I followed him into his offices. As I trailed him down the hall, we passed cubicle after cubicle, with actresses, singers, and other entertainers rehearsing. A little boy plunked loudly (and a little off key) on a piano in one of them. I followed Mr. Franco into his office at the end of the hall.

He told me to sit down, picked up two of my photos, and paced across the room a few times. He was a pleasant man with a kindly smile.

"Perry," he began, "you look good. And this sort of thing is really in demand. I can book you almost anyplace. But, if you want to make it big, you need a gimmick, something to make you stand out from the rest. A slogan—that's what you need!"

He paced some more.

"You're from—where—the South, aren't you?"

"Yes, from Louisiana."

"I've got it!" He waved his arms in an arch, describing a theater marquee. "We'll call you 'The South's Most Beautiful Boy.' That's perfect! I've already got you a booking," he said, moving toward his big desk, "the Jockey Club in Atlantic City." He sat down and began to write on some yellow paper. "They'll pay $125.00 a night."

I gasped. That was GOOD pay for 1959!

"OK, Per," Mr. Franco said, looking up from the yellow paper, "sign the contract right here."

I did.

"Now, Perry, be sure to phone me when you get back into town." He opened the door for me.

My head was full of new thoughts and thrills as I passed down the hall, hardly noticing the practicing actors or the plunking piano. The secretary screamed something past her adenoids as the door slammed behind me. But I didn't bother to ask her what. I was on my way to Atlantic City—The South's Most Beautiful Boy!

THE JOCKEY CLUB

The Jockey Club was the rowdiest nightclub in Atlantic City. It featured strippers, dirty comics, and unusual acts like mine. It was the raunchiest place I'd ever seen, and I'd seen some pretty raunchy places!

They would lock all the doors during one of the acts (to keep the police out), and then the men would throw money on the stage. The girl who did this act would pick up the bills in a way that cannot be described. It was really only a glorified strip joint, but I loved it. Lechers made up the audience each night. They were loaded, and we gleaned their wallets.

Then I moved on. My agent, Mr. Franco, booked me in clubs around the city. My title, The South's Most Beautiful Boy, got a lot of attention and loads of jobs for me.

THE CATSKILLS

Doors opened for me to go to the famous Catskill Mountains. The routine was one club after another, and lots of drinking in between. I began to notice that I didn't have much energy. Most of the places I was working were really dumps, but I worked one good one.

Fleishmann's was a fine place to work. It was a Hungarian Jewish town. I did part-time work as a hairdresser. One day I was doing a lady's hair when I noticed a tattoo on her arm. She saw me staring at it.

"That's my brand," she said, smiling. "The beast burned it on me—Hitler. You never saw one? Here, look." She thrust her arm up in my face. I looked at the faded blue marks, a kind of serial number of some sort.

"There," she continued, "now you've seen one. See the 'A'? That stands for Auschwitz. You heard of it? The Germans came in and shut everything down. They kicked in our door and shot my father. I saw it. Then they took me for a whore. That's when they put on this brand." She pointed at the blue marks again. "But I was lucky. I got away."

She was a beautiful, red-haired lady. She smiled and settled back in her chair.

"Just do something simple to it," she said, pointing to her head. I gave her what she really wanted, a fantastic, swooping hair-do! I called it "the Synagogue Sweep." She always asked for me when she came after that.

"She was branded," I thought silently. "So am I."

INTO THE TOMBS

The Jewel Box Revue was back. They were on Broadway now, for the first time. They had really made it. They were playing at Lowe's State Theatre.

**Perry as
"The South's Most Beautiful Boy"**

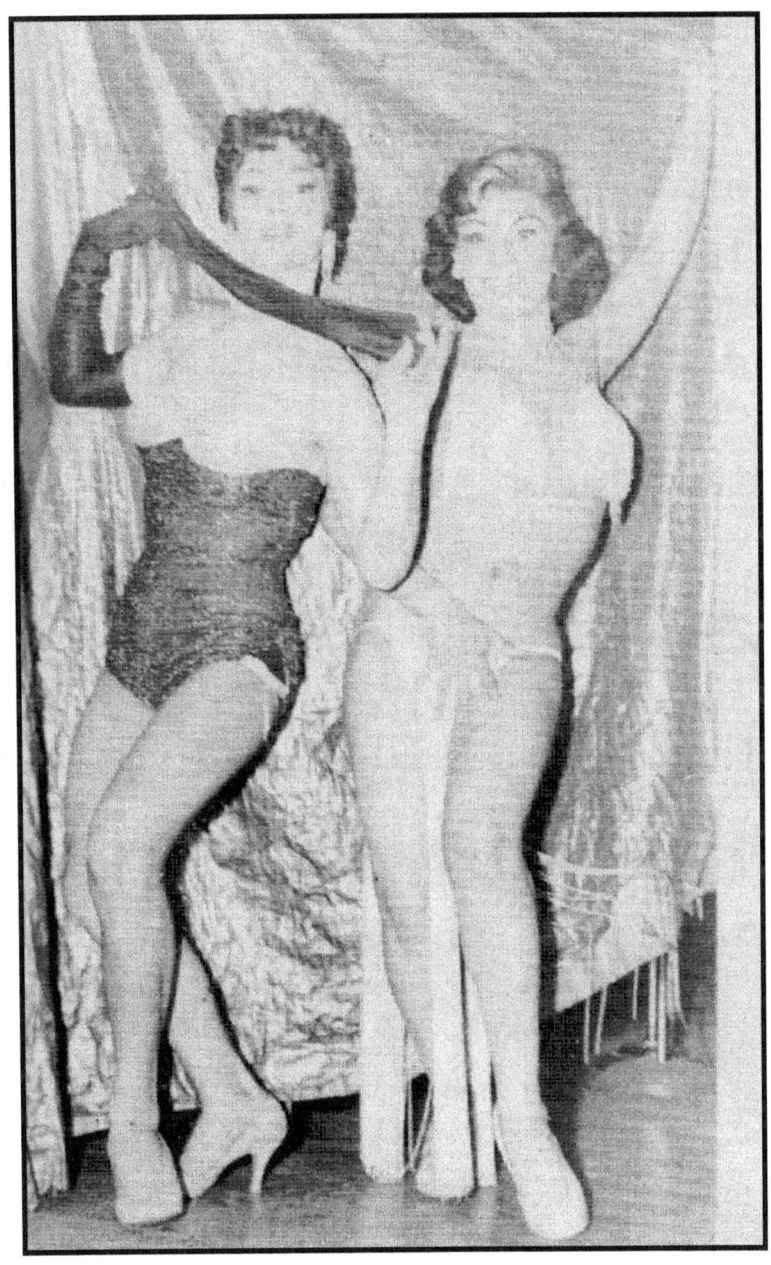

Perry and Transsexual Co-Worker

I was tired of running around. The security of The Jewel Box was what I wanted now. I wished I had never left them. I would see Danny Brown and beg him to give me my job back. I'd go first thing in the morning.

That night the big costume ball at Manhattan Center was being held. It was a once-a-year event. Prizes for the best get-ups were given, liquor flowed, bands played. Anyone who was "anybody" was there.

Hundreds of people were swaying to the sounds of music. I was just getting into the swing of it. Suddenly a whistle blew. A metallic voice crackled over a bullhorn, "Stay right where you are!"

Someone in politics had decided to "clean up the city." I was one of those who got "cleaned." They swept up 143 people. I was one of them—in the wrong place at the wrong time.

They whizzed us through the streets in huge paddy wagons, the kind you see in movies but never expect to ride in. In a few minutes we were herded like goats into the police station, through corridor after corridor, down, farther and farther, into the dank, oppressive vaults of the underground jail cells of the New York Police Department. They called it "The Tombs." I could see why!

They fingerprinted me, ripped off my clothes, sent me through a shower, and sprayed me with a pesticide. I was sick, literally in the tombs—The South's Most Beautiful Boy!

5
METAMORPHOSIS

We were locked in a row of cells. It was three tiers high, and almost a city block long. I was in a cell in the bottom tier. They threw us in with the most hardened criminals. My eyes gradually adjusted to the dim light. I was crammed in with five other queens. One of them was crying.

Now I knew why they called it The Tombs. In the cells on either side of us were the weirdest, most grotesque people I had ever laid eyes on. Pimps, whores, drug addicts with pincushion imprints on their arms, festering with pus. One had a huge abscess, the size of a lemon, on his arm, where he had missed the vein with his rusty needle.

A drunk in the tier above us vomited through the bars. The rancid brown liquid splashed on the cement floor in front of our cell.

Inmates were milling about in the area just outside. A huge man popped his head against the bars and ogled at me.

He had a large, jagged blue scar across his face, pulling down one corner of his mouth.

"Hey, baby," he growled, "gimme your address and I'll look you up when we get out."

I shuddered. I was glad there were bars between us.

In the next cell was a black queen. He had looked so beautiful in his black ritual robe and feathered headband a few hours before. Now he was lost and dejected, standing there in prison overalls. The grand irony of it was the bright red polish still on his toe nails.

CLANG! CLANG! CLANG!

The doors opened abruptly. A cop yelled out, "All right, girls, you got *one* call. You better make it count!" We scrambled for the phones.

Who would I call? My mind fumbled over an imaginary list. After scratching off five or six people, I decided to phone my ex-boss, Charles, who owned the beauty salon on Central Park West. He was surprised to hear my voice. Within an hour he had me bailed out.

As we walked out into the street, he looked at me in surprise.

"Perry, you're yellow! You're bright yellow!" He rushed

me to the hospital.

THE HOSPITAL

The doctor took one look at me and said, "Infectious Hepatitis. Put him in isolation, third floor." I had Yellow Jaundice.

By now I was so weak I could hardly lift my arms. I had been a male nurse in the service, so I knew how serious this illness was. Death was close, and I felt almost too weak to fight it.

That night I woke from my delirium several times. I saw them wheel four bodies out of the ward. Later I learned we were in the midst of a Hepatitis epidemic.

Weeks passed into months. I was getting stronger. The doctors told me my liver was regenerating itself. I read Leon Uris' *Mila-18*, a popular novel about the Warsaw ghetto in Hitler's Germany. Then, very slowly, I was able to get up and walk a little.

One morning I woke up looking right into Tom's face. I had written him off months before, after hearing that conversation with his mother through the kitchen door. He had found out from the beauty salon where I was. It was great to see him again!

Tom told me how much he had missed me. He had a

falling out with his mother, had given her back the car, and here he was. He wanted to patch things up with me.

TINA

Tom and I moved to Asbury Park, New Jersey, near the boardwalk. A light breeze blew in from the ocean every afternoon. Tom got a job selling shoes. We would take long walks along the beach when he got home from work. It was invigorating. There was a fabulous Chinese restaurant near our apartment. I loved to eat there. I felt my strength returning.

Then one day I received a letter from my cousin. She told me Dad was sick again. I hadn't talked with Mother for many months, but today I wanted to phone her. I was in a melancholy mood when I called. We both cried.

She confirmed my worst fears. Dad had taken a turn for the worse. He was even acting irrational. She said that he had gone to a tent revival two weeks before, and now he would talk about Jesus and read the Bible all day. She told me he sat in his favorite chair humming choruses and hymns for hours on end.

"He must be going insane," she went on. "He even told me he isn't afraid to die anymore. He keeps saying that Jesus loves him. Perry, I'm afraid. I think he's gone crazy. Please come home."

I was worried about Dad. It all kept going through my

mind—his talk about Jesus, the hymn singing, and all. It was so unlike him. I wanted to go home and take care of Mother, but I was afraid of alarming her with my sickly appearance. I decided to wait a few months until I was well.

On weekends Tom and I would go to the city to see a Broadway show or a movie. One afternoon we went to the west 70s to visit some old friends.

As we walked down the street, I saw a beautiful woman walking toward us. She looked a little like an old friend of mine named Tina. I looked again. It was Tina! But she was so feminine, her skin so soft, and she had breasts!

"Tina!" I cried, "How? What? You look FABULOUS! What did you do?"

He smiled and told me how he'd met a doctor who was giving him hormone shots and tablets. He'd had electrolysis on his face to remove his beard. And what was even more shocking—he was leaving for Casablanca in two weeks to have a sex-change operation. It was as if someone hit me with a sledge hammer!

"Tina, you've got to give me that doctor's name and address! This is what I've always wanted."

Tom shot a disapproving look at me. He liked me as I was. Later he told me he didn't want any changes.

My mind was made up, however. I fairly floated back to New Jersey that night. This was what I'd wanted all my life.

Nothing could stop me now.

HORMONES

I contacted Dr. Ritter the next day. He gave me an appointment, and, a few days later, I went to see him. He had a beautiful office on Fifth Avenue. The nurse greeted me. I filled out the necessary papers. She weighed me, and I sat down.

I was so nervous I strained to breathe. My heart felt as though it would leap from my throat.

Dr. Ritter entered the examination room. He was tall, with close-cropped hair on the sides of a bald head. He had the scrubbed, metallic look of a person who thinks in terms of numbers, equations, and machines.

He picked up a stethescope, walked toward me, and placed the cold end of it against my chest. I winced a little.

"Where is your home?" He asked. His voice was low, but had a crisp authority. A touch of some European accent was evident on the edges of the precise words he chose. "You mean here, in New York?"

"No. Where were you born and raised?"

"In Louisiana."

"I see. How did you find out about me?"

"My friend, Tina. She's been coming here."

"Yes, I know her." He turned and faced the wall. He took out a folder and wrote something in it. "And what do you want me to do for you?"

"I… I want hormone treatments. I want to be a woman."

"What makes you think you want to be a woman?" He still had his back to me. I briefly told him the story of my life, how I'd always wanted to be a woman.

He wrote again in the folder. Then he sat on a chair in front of me and looked me square in the eyes. His penetrating gaze seemed to be probing my inner mind.

"You know," he continued, "the transsexual's plight is really very sad. For years psychiatrists have tried to change the mind to fit the body. But this is not the answer to the gender identity question. Science has discovered a better solution through testing and experimentation. We now know that through extensive hormone therapy, and conversion surgery, we can shape the body to fit the mind. However, because this phase of medicine is in the infant stage, we are still experimenting. You must therefore give a great deal of thought to this before we begin."

I thought a moment before replying.

"Dr. Ritter, I've been thinking about this for the past twenty years. My mind is made up. I want to be a woman."

He wrote something else on the chart, looked up, and continued speaking. "Very well, Perry Desmond. We will start your hormone treatment immediately."

He opened a shiny metal drawer and took out a syringe. With a pair of sterile forceps, he picked a long needle out of a pan and adjusted it on the end of the syringe.

Then he grinned. It was a curious, humorless smile. "You will need to bend over just a little, Perry Desmond."

I hardly felt the needle. My mind was filled with thoughts of my life-long dream. It was about to become a reality, at last, thanks to Dr. Ritter.

I came back to the doctor's office every week, taking the bus through the tunnel, into New York City. First, I would have an examination, then my hormone shot. Then I'd meet a friend for lunch, and we'd go shopping. Tom would give me money each week for all this, but it was getting difficult to stretch his salary.

I took a part-time job at an elegant beauty salon in Allenhurst, New Jersey. It was a wealthy area and the pay was good. I needed it now, especially since Dr. Ritter had sent me to a psychiatrist. The psychiatric examination was just routine. Dr. Ritter had all his patients go through it to see if they were stable enough to undergo the treatments. Everyone who had hormone treatments and was contemplating a sex-change operation had to go.

The psychiatrist looked up over his glasses, from behind a cluttered desk, and fired a battery of questions at me. "How long have you wanted to be a woman?"

"How old are you?"

"What kind of work do you do?"

"Have you ever tried to commit suicide?"

"Is there any history of mental illness in your family?"

I must have answered them all correctly, because he signed some papers, handed them to me, and told me to pay the girl at the desk. He didn't even look up, but began fumbling through the mess of papers on his desk. He was a nervous, sallow person. Have you ever seen someone who looked like he'd have bad breath if you got close to him? That was the distinct impression I got from him as I stood there.

"If I'd told him I wanted to be a monkey, I'll bet he'd have signed papers letting them graft some fur and a tail on me," I thought, a smile crossing my face as I paid the receptionist.

CAT ON A HOT TIN ROOF

My body started responding to the hormones. My breasts and hips began to enlarge, and my face took on a luminous glow, as though you had rubbed just a bit of cocoa butter into it.

Soon everyone noticed the difference. A girl at the beauty

salon asked, "What did you do to look so good?" The overall effect was startling. I looked more like a woman than ever in my life, even without makeup. People on the street never stared at me now. I looked like a woman, even when wearing men's clothing. I was pleased with my new "identity."

Then the bad effects of the hormones began. Dr. Ritter had asked me to keep a day-by-day diary of my feelings and actions. I would often read the notes of previous days when making a new entry. It was then that I saw how erratic I was acting and feeling. It was as if I were a ping-pong ball— bouncing back and forth, from man to woman and back again. And the ping-pong table was my own brain!

I began taking out all my anxieties and hostilities on Tom. He could no longer do anything right in my eyes. Nothing, not even the new TV and car he bought me, was pleasing. I started feeling strange toward him. He wanted sex all the time, and the hormones had killed all my desires. I felt like a neutered animal.

Tom began seeing the girl downstairs, sneaking behind my back. By now the hormones had my emotions completely twisted. I didn't want sex, but I didn't want him seeing her either.

One night he sneaked down the fire escape after he thought I was asleep. Later he stole back up and was taking a shower. My emotions were boiling. I went to the kitchen and got the biggest pot I could find, taking it into the bathroom.

It was like *Psycho*; I ripped back the shower curtain and started letting him have it with the pot—again, and again, and again—over the head and back. It's a wonder I didn't really hurt him. I was wild, insane, disoriented, like a cat on a hot tin roof!

Once my system got used to the hormones, however, I settled into the "normal" routines of my new-found womanhood.

DADDY

Now I was in a depression again. I was getting homesick. It was the old, familiar yearning for New Orleans and my family. I decided to phone Mother.

"Hello," the voice on the other end answered.

"Who is *this?*"

"Perry, this is your Daddy!"

"Daddy, how are you feeling?"

"Great, son! Great!"

"Wow!" I thought, "That doesn't sound like *my* Daddy!"

"Is Mother home?" I continued.

"Yes, I'll get her for you, son. Take care. I'm praying for

you."

I could hear him put the receiver down and call Mother. She was right, I thought, he was so happy sounding—he *must* be going off the deep end! I just *couldn't* picture him praying for me!

Mother got on the line and asked when I was coming home. She didn't know about the hormones and the complete change in my appearance. I told her about it, that this was what I'd called about, and that I couldn't come back home now.

"But why not?" she cried.

"Mother, I'm under doctor's care. I'm taking hormone treatments. Soon I'll have sex-change surgery, like Christine Jorgenson. Mother, at last I'm going to be a woman!"

There was a long silence on the other end of the line. Her voice sounded strained when she answered, "Well, that seems nice, son." I knew that there were other people in the room, and she couldn't say what she really felt.

"But, Mother, Tom and I are coming back to New Orleans. Oh, Mother, I miss you all so much. I'll come back as soon as I can." I burst into uncontrollable tears.

When I had regained some of my composure, I told her I would phone her when I arrived. I hung up the phone. "I guess I'm going home after all," I mused.

RAPE AND RIP-OFF

Tom and I got an apartment on top of the Old French Opera House, a strip joint on Bourbon Street. It felt good to be home. The apartment was on the second floor; our balcony hung out over the patio. The strippers would change their clothes down there, in the slave quarter. You could see them running almost nude between the acts.

I got a job at a beauty salon. Then one day, while I was at work, Tom brought a sixteen-year-old girl he had picked up in the Jackson Square to the apartment. He raped her brutally. Someone from the club below phoned me, and I rushed home to find the place surrounded by police cars, sirens blaring and lights flashing. Just as I got there, they led Tom out in handcuffs and shoved him into one of the cars. Later one of the detectives told me the story.

I phoned a lawyer I knew and got Tom out of jail. The next day, while I was at work, Tom left, taking everything... except the dirty sheets on my bed. Those two sheets were all I had to show for my years of work, and all the money I had made.

I sat on the mattress and cried. I knew Tom was no longer responsible for his actions. The increasing amounts of drugs he'd been taking had made his mind like Swiss cheese. Later his mother committed him to an asylum.

I just sat there crying. Then, suddenly, I began to laugh. I was free! My body was quite feminine now. Most of my beard had been removed by electrolysis. Besides, I was the only boy in New Orleans with breasts! I had it made!

Sitting there on the bed, I decided to go back to the most lucrative type of work I knew—hustling. I fixed things up a little in the apartment and went out to buy a new "uniform," a "Jezebel" push-up bra, a black mini skirt, and a low-cut, black ruffled blouse.

In those days female impersonation was against the law, but I had no trouble with the police. They all thought I was just one of the "working girls" on Bourbon Street. They had never seen a boy with breasts. In fact, some of the other prostitutes were jealous of the new "girl" in town.

BABY DUKE

I teamed up with a young girl named Marilyn. She had left the Catholic convent, where she'd been preparing to become a nun, only one week before I met her. I introduced her to the world of prostitution. We would pick up a rich "John" and do a "three-way" with him. We made more money this way.

Soon I had enough money to open my own beauty salon. It was on St. Phillip Street. Most of the prostitutes and show girls became my customers.

I bleached my hair snow white, bought some new outfits,

and started hitting the bars, looking for a lover.

I was about half drunk the night I met Baby Duke. Through the haze of smoke in the bar, I saw him. He looked a lot like James MacArthur, Helen Hayes' son. He noticed me staring at him, came over, and asked me to dance. Baby was from North Carolina.

He had money, and was attractive and young, an unusual combination. I couldn't let it pass me by. He wanted me to get silicone injections to further enlarge my breasts, and to complete my sex-change surgery. He said he would help me. We moved in together at the outskirts of the French Quarter, a place where no one knew me.

I became a "typical" housewife, my mini-skirt replaced by cotton dresses, my bleached hair dyed back to its natural shade. I began cooking and keeping house for Baby Duke.

The woman next door had five children. I started baby-sitting one of her little boys. Soon I had him all the time. I told everyone I was his mother when I took him out shopping or to the movies. My housewife charade was nearly perfect.

MY TRUE NATURE

Baby was showering me with gifts now—a new car, an RCA entertainment center, credit cards, you name it! But he was gone most nights, working a graveyard shift from nine to five in the morning.

I should have been happy. This was what I'd always thought I wanted, to get out of the night-life mess and settle down. But, instead of being content, I was bored to death. Baking cakes and washing dishes began to seem like a drag. Baby Duke was gone every night, too. I wanted the "old feeling" of excitement. I started going back to the bars. That's when I met Wayne.

My friend Cherry, a hooker, and I were sitting at the end of the bar one night. She was telling me about her new boy friend.

"Here he is!" she exclaimed, pointing toward a tall, dark man coming in our direction. He had a friend with him. The friend looked a lot like Baby, only better. His name was Wayne, and, as we talked, I felt that *this* was the man I'd always wanted.

Wayne worked on a job that kept him away on an offshore oil rig for two weeks. Then he'd come back for a week. I began seeing him every night during the weeks he was off. Baby didn't know a thing about it. I went with both of them like this for a whole year.

Then one day Wayne told me I had to give up Baby if I wanted to see him again. He flashed a large wad of money. "I have enough cash for us to get our own apartment," he exclaimed triumphantly.

I didn't want to give up the security I had, but he was forcing me to choose. I chose to go with him.

When I returned home that night, I put the car keys on the mantle and left a note:

Baby—it's best this way,
          Love, Perry

Wayne and I moved in together and had a wonderful "honeymoon." Later I heard that Baby Duke had started drinking, cut his wrists, and later lost everything we'd accumulated together. But I was so calloused by then that it really didn't bother me much.

Looking back, I realize how perverted I was becoming. Part of me enjoyed the thought of Baby slitting his wrists and mourning over me.

Why did I want to hurt the men who loved me? Perhaps I was "getting back" at all the big hulks who taunted and teased me as a teenager. Later I even made several of my lovers tattoo "I LOVE PERRY" (encircled with a heart) on their chests, thus branding them for life. The sadistic part of me cherished all this.

Then Daddy died.

6

THE

EGYPTIAN READING ROOM

I leaned over the coffin. He was dead; there was no doubt about it. But there was a slight smile on his face. "Just one of the mortician's tricks," I thought.

But my eyes kept drifting back to his mouth. It *was* smiling. I was overcome with tears. Why did I feel such grief? I'd thought I didn't love him.

The funeral was about to begin, so I made my way to the restroom to wash the tears from my face. I stopped myself at the women's and went in the men's. Going in the women's restroom was a habit by now, but I might have shocked someone, because today I was dressed as a man.

Once in the restroom, I looked at myself in the mirror. My "new" nose was quite different from before. My mind shot back to the hospital, the long needles piercing my flesh beneath my eyes, the hammer and chisel, and the spurting blood. But it was all worth it. I had the beautiful, up-turned nose of a woman now.

In fact, I looked exactly like a woman, a woman in men's clothing. I had cut my hair shorter for the funeral. It was plastered down with hair spray. I had bought a blue suit, white shirt, and tie. But they gave me the odd, incongruous look of a lesbian dressed like a man.

I walked back down the hall, into the nave of the church. Relatives and friends were already seated. Someone whispered in my ear, asking me to be a pall bearer. I refused, remembering all the hated funerals I had assisted at as an altar boy. Another thought flashed through my mind—would my funeral be held in this church?

They ushered me to the front pew with my family.

All eyes turned toward me. I felt naked and in the spotlight. I realized how weird I looked in that lumpy suit, my long hair swept back in a ducktail . . . and my "new" nose. I could feel what they were thinking. It would be good to get away from them all and be back home on Bourbon Street.

I fled there as quickly as possible after the funeral. Thoughts of Daddy filled my mind with a strange mellowness as I drove back.

INTO BLACK ARTS

The Haunted House was a perfect place, just what I wanted for my next beauty salon. It was an ancient, pre-Civil War mansion. Madame Lalurie had been a very wealthy land owner when she built it. She reportedly kept scores of slaves chained in the attic. There were tales of her pushing them off the third story into a well in the patio. They said she did it for amusement. After her death, people heard screams in that attic. Doors opened and closed by themselves. The mansion was famous.

I rented the lower level of this beautiful old house. At first I laughed at the rumors. But I grew less skeptical when I actually saw doors open and close a couple of times. One customer told me it was the devil. Was it? "Of course not," I told myself. "No one believes in the devil anymore. It's just the way the house was built . . . gravity . . . that sort of thing."

I was getting silicone injections in my breasts and hips. This was adding to my feminine good looks. I was literally pouring the money that was coming from the salon into my body. I had become a silicone "addict."

Why wasn't I happy? I had everything I'd wanted, but I was miserable inside. None of my friends had any answers. They were as confused as I was. I don't know why I didn't go to a psychiatrist. Maybe I was too turned-off by the one I'd met in New York City.

Then I turned to astrology. I had been reading my horoscope in the papers for years. I began to think, "Maybe there's really something to it. Maybe I can get guidance from it."

I started collecting astrology books. One of my customers was a very wealthy woman. She asked me if I'd like to go to a fortune-teller with her one afternoon. I went, and had my palm and cards read. Among other things, the reader told me I had psychic ability. She said the occult would play an important part in my future.

Right away I began asking the customers in my beauty salon what their signs were. Then I made some charts for them, for free, just to practice. I bought an Ephemeris, a book which shows all the locations of the planets at any given time. I really got into it. Soon astrology became the most important thing in my life.

BLACK LIGHTS

Wayne was drinking heavily now. He would come in after two weeks of work, and spend his whole pay check in the bars. It was just like when I was a child. Only now, I was Mother, and he was Daddy. We re-lived all the horrors of those early days of Daddy's drunkenness. But I was so much in love with Wayne I didn't really mind.

One of my hairdressers was into psychedelic drugs quite

heavily. He started trying to get me to drop some LSD too. Late one afternoon I took my first "hit." The room whirled. The walls collapsed and expanded like an accordion. The letters on a TIME Magazine lifted and shivered several inches above the book. It was a "good trip." I loved it. From then on, I smoked pot nearly every day, staying high for twenty-four hours at a stretch.

When Wayne came back, I turned him on to drugs as well, hoping it would help curb his drinking.

We fixed the apartment up with "day glow" posters, black light, and a whole new set of records featuring Jefferson Airplane, Dr. John the Night Tripper, The Grateful Dead, and others. I used to lie on the bed in a mountain of colored pillows listening to them, tripping on the drugs I'd taken.

THE AGE OF AQUARIUS

A prime location opened up on Bourbon Street, and I moved the salon there. I was doing astrological charts at home now. In fact, more and more of my time was being taken up in this way, as I lost interest in the beauty business. I was making much more money on the charts, and it was far more interesting to me than fooling with some woman's hair.

I finally sold the beauty salon and leased a thirteen-room building in the heart of the French Quarter, right on Bourbon Street. I was about to embark on my most fantastic venture—

an occult conglomeration of shops that I called The Age of Aquarius. Money poured in from the day it opened.

One of the most popular features of the complex was The Egyptian Reading Room. It was a large room, made to resemble the Egyptian desert. Sand covered the floor, the solar system was painted on the ceiling. A tent was erected at each of the room's four corners.

Readers were in the tents, each one having his own specialty. One read tarot cards, one was a crystal ball gazer, another was a palm reader, and the fourth told fortunes with a regular deck of cards. For $3.00 you could have your choice of readings, which lasted from 10 to 15 minutes. The astrological charts started at $7.50 each. Money was rolling in—and I was miserable.

SOMETHING MISSING

Why was I so depressed? Maybe it was Wayne's heavy drinking and carousing that troubled me.

It was a Saturday night and The Age of Aquarius was packed with people. I had just had double injections of silicone in both breasts. I had on a special brassiere that the doctor had given me to hold my breasts in place until the silicone settled. He told me to be very careful not to jar them.

Wayne had stormed out earlier that day, angry at me for

Perry at his Desk in "The Age of Aquarius"

spending so much money on these injections.

"How selfish," I thought, considering all the money he spent on booze!

My thoughts were drifting to the confrontation we would have when he came home the next morning. Lately he had started beating me. He had even threatened to kill me a few times.

I had just seated a customer in the palm reader's tent, and was walking toward the door, when Wayne pounced on me. I fell backwards on the sand-covered floor. My breasts, very tender yet from the injections, felt as though they were being ripped off as he dived on me, slugging me again and again in the face.

"You dirty faggot," he shouted. "It's all your fault! If I hadn't met you my life wouldn't be so messed up!"

"Wayne, stop! Stop!" I screamed.

"You faggot! You faggot!" he yelled, beating me harder and harder on the floor of The Egyptian Reading Room.

A man bolted through the door. Clasping his arms around Wayne's neck, he pulled him off me. Betty, the girl in the gift shop, had called for the beat cops. They swarmed in now, pulling Wayne up from the floor. He was writhing like a wild animal. It took all four of the cops to hold him.

Somebody helped me up. I was shaking like a leaf. A

policeman asked if I wanted him booked.

"If you let me go, I'll leave this town and you'll never see me again!" Wayne yelled.

I nodded to the police to let him loose. They took him out into the street. I watched through the window as he melted into the pool of faces on Bourbon Street. He was gone from my life.

THE SPACE CAPSULE

It took me a few days for my face and body to recover from the beating Wayne had given me. As I recuperated, I began thinking that I never wanted to be "hung up" on one person again. I would play the field, be loose, enjoy myself. Soon I was feeling better.

As usual, I began this new phase of my life by going out to buy clothes, only this time they were *really* expensive. I also went back to my old routine of going with a bunch of guys at the bars. But I was beginning to get tired of that. That's when I came up with the idea of the space capsule.

There were two little-used office rooms and a bathroom at the back of the Age of Aquarius complex. I decided to convert them. I took hundreds of boxes of aluminum foil, crumpled them, and stapled the foil to the walls and ceiling. Then I had a water bed built into one of the corners. I put in a movie projector to show porno films. Colored lights were arranged to produce a fantastic effect, glittering off of the crumpled foil.

I started throwing parties in the Space Capsule. Almost every night we would smoke hash until we were out of our minds. It always ended in a sex orgy, the movie playing out scenes on the wall milder than what was going on in the room.

It wasn't long until even this left me unsatisfied. What *did* I want? I wasn't sure anymore. Maybe I'd be happy if I had the sex-change surgery. I'd put it off for various reasons before. Now I was ready.

7

THE WITCH'S PACT

I was bound up in the occult by now. I had my fortune told two and three times a day. I would plot my horoscope over and over.

Finally, in desperation, I went to a witch. It was a small shop off of Decatur Street. I opened the door, and the first thing that caught my eye was a coffin in the middle of the floor. I looked up at the walls. They were lined with bottles full of love and hate potions, and various other ingredients for casting spells: bat eyes, toad stools, and other such condiments.

Turning to the right, I saw a shelf of books on the occult, most of which I already had. A cat ran between my legs. I jumped back.

As I made my way toward the back of the room, I caught my first glimpse of Karla. I had read about her in the newspapers, but had never met her in person. She was famous all over New Orleans for her ability to cast spells.

She looked up and smiled. I couldn't help but think how attractive she was—black hair, white skin, and deep, shadowy eyes. I felt as though something else lived behind those eyes, looking out at me.

"Hello, I'm Perry. I need some help."

"Most people who come here do," she said, smiling. "What's your problem?"

I told her of my life, with its series of dramatic successes and equally dramatic failures. I told her of my many love affairs, and how my last lover, Wayne, had left me; how sick I'd been, lonely, and without hope.

"What do you want now, money or love?" she asked. "Both," I answered quickly.

She opened a book that lay on the table in front of her, thumbed through the pages, stopping with her finger resting on the text. "What you need, Perry, is Solomon's Seal."

She closed the book and went to the other side of the room. Reaching into a drawer, she took out a piece of brown parchment.

"You know, you don't get anything for nothing," she continued. "Sign the name of the person you love at the top of this sheet and your own name at the bottom."

It was so dark in the room I could hardly see. I scratched Wayne's name on the top and mine on the line at the bottom.

She took the "pact" and sealed it in an envelope, saying, "Don't open this. Don't read it. It's sealed now. Put it under your mattress, near the head of your bed. Everything will work out as you desire."

Taking the envelope in my hand, I stumbled out of the dimly lit room, down the street, toward The Age of Aquarius.

A confidence filled me that I hadn't felt for weeks. I slept soundly with the witch's pact under my mattress. Not once did I think of her words, "You know, you don't get anything for nothing."

THE BIG STEP

Dr. Murphy Seeling was a plastic surgeon in New York. I phoned him long distance, telling him that I had been under hormone treatment for more than ten years, and that I was now ready for the sex-change surgery.

He spoke very reassuringly, "Perry, you know, now we do the surgery in two stages. The first step involves total castration. I can do that for you on August eleventh. Can you be in Yonkers then?"

"Yes," I said, without hesitation, "I'll be there." "Good,"

Dr. Seeling continued, "We'll discuss the second phase of the operation when you get here."

I was so excited! I phoned everyone and told them... including my mother. By now she had reconciled herself to the idea. She even promised me she'd come and run The Age of Aquarius while I was away—a promise she kept.

That afternoon the phone rang. It was Wayne, speaking very slowly and from what seemed like very far away. "Perry, I love you. Can I come home?"

My heart melted. The witch's pact had worked! He was coming back! I told him that I had made an appointment for surgery, and was going in on August eleventh. He said, "Good, I'll go with you."

The witch's pact had *really* worked!

CRAZY LARRY

Wayne returned. He told me what he'd been doing since he left, how he'd become a male hustler in Texas. He had teamed up with a fellow called Crazy Larry. The two of them would get themselves picked up by a rich homosexual. When they'd get to the man's house, Crazy Larry would pull out a pistol, point it at the man's head and say, "Give us all your money, or you're a dead queer."

Something hurt inside me when I thought of Wayne doing all this. But I attributed it to the drugs he'd been taking. And I knew that Crazy Larry really *was* crazy. This man took so many drugs his skin crawled.

Wayne related to me how they went to one man's house. Larry took out his gun and shot the homosexual in the shoulder. Then he turned the gun on Wayne, shouting, "I ought to kill you, too! I think you're a fag! You've lived with one in New Orleans long enough!"

Wayne threw a pillow in Larry's face and rushed out the door. That was when he had phoned me, asking if he could come back.

COUNT DOWN

I felt marvelous as I spoke on the phone late that afternoon. "Eastern Airlines? Yes? That's right, two reservations . . . Mr. and Mrs. Wayne Littlefield. That's right L-I-T-T-L-E-F-I-E-L-D. Yes, for next Friday, at 10:00 A.M. Thank you." I hung up the receiver, feeling very proud of myself. I had finally taken the "big"step to becoming the woman I'd always felt I was.

Just when everything was going so well, leave it to Wayne to mess up! The night before we were to leave, he and I got in a huge fight. In a complete rage, I called the police and had him arrested. They found marijuana on him and threw him in jail. It took hundreds of dollars to bail him out.

Wayne was mad at me, but no madder than I was at myself for taking him back after he was bailed out. Nothing was going to stop me from having my operation, not even Mother, pleading with me to reconsider the night before we left. Her sister had died two days before, and she tried to get me to stay for the funeral.

That night I also found out that one of my best fortune tellers had been stealing customers, planned to open his own reading room, and wouldn't be back to work.

Thinking back, I realize that God Himself had placed all these obstacles in my path to keep me from getting the operation. But I was determined to have my *own* way . . . at any cost! No matter who it hurt!

The hotel room was beautiful; the juliet balcony overlooked the city of New York. I got up early that morning and went out there to think.

As I looked down over the city, people were scurrying below like small insects. I thought, "How strange. Those people spend their whole lives running about in this concrete maze, never seeing a field, a cow, or a river—how strange and useless their lives are—just running here and there in all that traffic."

Then I turned and looked at Wayne, asleep on the bed.

"What do I have to look forward to with him?" I wondered. "Will our life be just another series of beatings, arrests, and drunken brawls?" Our lives seemed as useless as those of the people crawling on the pavement below, but I shoved the thought out of my mind and went into the other room to phone the hospital and tell them that I'd arrived in New York.

The nurse was glad I'd phoned. The surgery had been moved up—two days earlier than scheduled—because the doctor had to be away. I was to enter surgery at 4:00 P.M. that very afternoon.

Suddenly the shock hit me. This was it! There was no turning back.

I ran to the bed and shook Wayne. "Wake up! Wake up! It's today! The surgery is today! We have to get ready. I'm going to be castrated at four o'clock . . . Oh, Wayne, I'm so nervous!"

"What are you afraid of?" he asked pulling me over to him by the hand. "This is what you always wanted, isn't it?"

A thought flashed through my mind—"Is it? Is it really?" But I pushed it down into my subconscious, and rang for coffee.

THE OPERATION

We phoned for a cab and left for the hospital. It was a long drive. The fare was outrageous, but I didn't care. As we pulled up in front of the hospital, I thought there must have been a mistake. It was a shabby-looking place, like an abortion mill in a grade "B" movie. But the driver assured us that this was the right place.

We walked into the lobby and I checked in. A nurse had me sit in the waiting room for a few minutes. I glanced at myself in the mirror on the waiting room door. I had on a two-piece, emerald green outfit, all my jewelry, my gold charm bracelet, several rings, and black, patent leather shoes, trimmed in gold. I looked every bit like a smart, sophisticated woman. No one would have believed I was a man coming to be castrated.

A nurse came down to the lobby. Six women were there waiting with me. She looked us over. It made me grin to think that she couldn't pick out the man in the group!

I made the first move. "I'm Perry Desmond," I said. She remarked on how attractive I looked, and led Wayne and I into another room.

"You were the last one in the bunch I would have picked as the transsexual! You've really succeeded in making the change," she confided, as we walked down the corridor. Wayne followed me, and we sat down to fill in the necessary papers. I laughed as I came to the block marked "sex?" So did Wayne.

Dr. Seeling was world-renowned, not only for sex-change operations, but for his ability to remold faces with silicone as well. Many Hollywood stars flew to New York to have his skilled hands erase the tell-tale lines from their faces. I decided that this was a perfect opportunity to have my face redone, too. I told the nurse, and she gave me some more forms to fill out, absolving Dr. Seeling from any responsibility for side effects that might come from the silicone injections. Silicone had not been on the market long. Its effects were really unknown. This much was certain, however, silicone is extremely dangerous to inject into human tissues. I wanted it badly enough to risk my life. I filled in the forms and handed them to the nurse.

I had spoken with Dr. Murphy Seeling on the phone. I had imagined him as a tall, dark movie star, like Warren Beatty. Instead, he was a short, blue-eyed blond.

The operating room had an antiseptic smell. The nurse helped me onto the table. I lay there in a white robe as she sprayed a strong germicide of some kind around the room. Dr. Seeling lifted up my gown and placed a sterile sheet with a round hole in it over my genitals.

He took off the gloves he had on and put on another pair. The nurse entered with a large tray of needles. They were longer than any I had ever seen.

"Perry, this may sting a little," he said as he injected the first needle. I was glad they had me tied down. I strained back against the straps as sharp, piercing pains shot up in wave after wave, exploding in my brain.

He followed that injection with another. Once I looked down and saw the needle. It looked six inches long. Sweat stood out on my forehead.

Then I began to feel the knife cutting into my flesh. "He said I wouldn't feel this," I thought, grinding my teeth and writhing in pain. "But, then, doctors and dentists always say that." It was the most dreadful experience of my life.

It seemed as though the operation went on for an eternity. It felt as if he had removed all my insides. It was a relief to hear him ask the nurse for sutures to close the incision.

I happened to glance down. It was a mistake. I saw what he was dropping into the stainless steel basin. My mind reeled.

He then moved toward my face. With the skill of a precision jeweler working on a delicate watch, he began injecting silicone into my face and cheeks. Then he took his fingers and molded the stuff beneath the surface of my skin.

"There. That does it," he said, looking at me with a smile. "Any time after ninety days, get back in touch with me and we'll complete the surgery. The nurse will give you a letter from me stating that you have undergone this surgery, and that you are now legally a woman."

Later, in my room, I looked at the letter. It read in part:

To Whom It May Concern:

This is to certify that on August 11, 1972, Perry Desmond underwent partial sex-change surgery, and is now to be considered female.

It is very important for this patient's psychological well being that she be considered and treated as a woman at all times.

If there are any questions, please do not hesitate to contact me.

Signed,

Murphy L. Seeling, M.D.

_____ Hospital

New York, New York

Wayne was waiting in the hall as I hobbled out of surgery. They wanted me to stay in the hospital, but I insisted on going home. I flew back to New Orleans one day later, against the doctor's orders.

Perry Desmond 1973 - After Massive Doses of Female Hormones, Plastic Surgery, Silicone Injections and Being Castrated . . .

"Professing Themselves To Be Wise - They Became Fools"

Romans 1:22

8

PLUCKED FROM THE FIRE

What a mistake! No sooner did we get back than I noticed an unusual swelling in my groin. The pain was unbearable. I couldn't even walk. I had to stay in bed all day.

What would I have done without Mother? She had stayed and taken care of The Age of Aquarius while Wayne and I were in New York. Now she was taking care of me.

The pain continued. I phoned the hospital and asked for their urologist. They gave me his name and I phoned his office and made an appointment for the next day.

"You did what?" the doctor asked, looking at my incisions. He seemed to be around seventy years old. He had never even heard of sex-change operations. He gazed in numb wonder at my surgery.

The doctor called in a nurse. "Look, look at this!" he shouted. "Just look at what the doctors of today do!" Then he turned to me. "There's nothing I can do for you. Go home and put an ice pack on it."

I had tried to get in contact with Dr. Seeling, but with no result. Now I tried again, but he was out of town. I decided to try the ice pack.

It did no good. After two days my abdomen was as hard as a rock and beginning to swell. Later I learned that the icepacks could easily have killed me.

"Hello! What do you want? Don't you know that I'm a very busy man?" It was Dr. Seeling returning my call. I was amazed at how harsh his voice sounded since I had paid him. It was so soothing before.

"Dr. Seeling," I screamed, "something is terribly wrong with me. I have a high fever, and my lower abdomen is hard and swollen. I went to a urologist at the hospital here. He told me to go home and put an ice bag on it. But it hasn't helped."

"An ice bag!" he yelled. "You get into a tub of hot water, and do it right now. Get rid of that doctor and get a *decent* urologist."

I got into the tub of hot water and sat there for a few minutes. Suddenly it felt as though my insides were bursting. I had developed a huge inner abcess, and the first doctor's advice of applying an ice bag was the worst thing I could have done!

I have never in my life experienced anything like what happened next. It felt like someone kicked me in the groin. The stitches popped open and a huge draft of blood and pus shot out into the tub. I screamed.

"What's wrong? What happened?" Mother gasped, entering the bathroom.

"I don't know! God! Oh, God! Help me, Mother!"

I got out of the tub and sat on the toilet. Bright red blood ran down into the water. I looked at it with horror and revulsion. Finally, I got up and hobbled into the bedroom to lie down.

"Why did I do this to myself? Why . . . oh why?" The horror of it tore through my mind in great depressing waves.

I had been on the mailing list of the Erickson Educational Foundation for years. They are an organization that works with transsexuals. I thought they might be able to help me, so I phoned them. They gave me the name and number of a urologist in New Orleans who had treated transsexuals. I phoned him, and he told me to come over right away.

His office was in a building next to a hospital. They put me in the examination room on a table, with my feet up in stirrups. I was alone there. I was afraid and began to cry. I felt I was going to die. All my old fears came back, the fear of loneliness, darkness, isolation, and the dread of dying. I began to sob.

Dr. Craft came into the room. "Hey stop! Don't cry," he said in a comforting way. Then he moved down to the end of the table to look at my incisions.

"Oh, come on. It's not all that bad," he said as he felt my abdomen. Then he looked up and said, "Well, I have good news for you. You're not going to die. You just have a very bad abcess. We'll drain it, pack you with gauze, and put you on antibiotics. In a few weeks you'll be as good as new."

I must have been in Dr. Craft's office fifty times in the next few weeks. He was interested in my case. He asked me a thousand questions. He wanted more information on what makes a transsexual tick. I told him as much as I knew. I was beginning to wonder myself!

WAYNE FLIPS OUT

Mother had been with me a month now. She had to go back to work. I was feeling better, so I urged her to do so.

No sooner had she left than Wayne started drinking heavily again. I had only been out of bed two days when we had the biggest knock-down, drag-out fight ever. He was totally spaced out. I hadn't realized, during my sickness, that he'd been doing so much dope.

As he screamed and cursed that day, it hit me—his mind was totally twisted by the pills, pot, and acid. I looked up at him, as he hovered over me in a rage. My thoughts skipped back seven years to the healthy, happy boy I first knew. What a shame that such a beautiful person could disintegrate so much in such a short time. Guilt rose in my heart; I realized much of it was my fault.

He stumbled across the room, banging furniture. Grabbing an expensive lamp, he dashed it into a thousand pieces against the fireplace. He began to scream. "Just give me some money and I'll split, you bitch!" His drug-dead eyes wandered wildly around the room.

I had been through this so many times—it was an instant replay. Reaching into my purse, I pulled out a roll of bills, the entire day's receipts from The Age of Aquarius, throwing them at him across the foot of the bed. He lunged for the money, cramming the bills into his pockets like a scavenger.

The door slammed behind him. I could hear him bouncing from one wall to the other in the hall, falling, stumbling, and cursing down the stairs. From the street, he screamed back up at me, as I stood in the window, "Don't worry, you won't die! You're too rotten, you ____!" I could hear his cursing grow fainter as he stumbled off down the street.

I lay there, alone in my room, surrounded by my coveted possessions. I had ruined him, just like all the other boys I'd known. "I get these boys caught in my web, only to destroy them, like a Black Widow spider," I thought. But tonight was different. I loved Wayne. We had made such great plans. Now the future looked hopeless. I destroyed these men because secretly I hated them. Deep down, I loathed all men: my father—Coach Koenig—the boys at school who teased me— Jack, who first made me do it to him—Tom, who deceived me—all the men who had "messed me over" through the years. This was my way of getting even, by leading them into drugs and perversion.

But there was one thing wrong with my game — it hurt me as badly as it hurt them — or worse. I lay there, limp, fatigued, alone, and devastated. My life had been a surrealistic nightmare, a Salvador Dali painting — or, better, like one of Andy Warhol's trashy, commercial movies.

I went to the bathroom. I glanced at myself in the mirror. Was this the chubby little face that had once shone from under a Buster Brown hat? My eyes were sunk back in blackened sockets. The silicone pockets in my cheeks looked ludicrous, like walnuts shoved up inside my mouth. My "reshaped" nose looked more like Bob Hope's than a woman's. Wrinkles and lines creased the edges of my eyes and mouth. My long hair, in great tangled masses, set it all off. . . wrong! It was like the incredible face of an actor. Only I couldn't take the makeup off. It was *me!*

I looked down at the marks on my wrists, where I had slit them. Each scar had its own story. The first one, when I had been in despair after a fight with my lover, the night when the first Americans had landed on the Moon. The second, when my lover had caught me with another man. The third, after a horrible fight. Each time it had been the same—my current lover had left me, and I had cut my wrists in despair.

I knew by now that wrist-cutting is a hard way to kill yourself. Too hard. I opened the medicine cabinet and took out the Nembutals. This would be easier. I swallowed the entire contents of the bottle.

I went to the kitchen to make myself a cup of hot tea to dissolve the pills more quickly. Then I got out all my scrapbooks while the water was heating. I decided to burn them. That way no one would be hurt looking at them later.

Sitting down to drink the tea, I began thumbing through the books, starting at the beginning.

There was a photo of me as a "quiz kid," a child prodigy. What a laugh!

There I was on Christmas Eve, straddling my new girl's bike. I turned the page, and there was Aunt Edna smiling out at me. It was taken just before she died.

The photos and clippings of me as a cheerleader were on the following pages.

I put down that album and picked up another. There it was—my first professional "drag" picture. What an appropriate word, I thought, this kind of life really *has* been a drag!

Now the drug was beginning to take effect. I gazed at the album through the growing fog in my mind. I could barely see the photo of Ed Rishard and I in the middle of Bourbon Street, during Mardi Gras, surrounded by throngs of people. We were dressed as Burt Lancaster and Gina Lollabrigida in the movie, "Trapeze." Everyone had commented on how much I looked like her. I should have; I'd taken hours on the makeup.

My head fell to one side, the album slipping from my lap. I shook my head and looked down at it. It had fallen open to a photo of myself, Sammy Davis, Jr., and the cast of the Jewel Box Revue.

I got up, stumbled, and fell on the floor.

Something was tickling my face. My hand brushed at it. Back it came. By the third or fourth time, I realized it was a fly. I sat up and coughed.

"I'm not dead!" It hit me like a bolt of lightning. "Or maybe I am dead, and this is hell!" The thought made me laugh, but I stopped short as a feeling of nausea filled my stomach. I got up, holding the wall, and made my way across the strewn pile of albums and photos, toward the bathroom. I didn't make it. A dark brown stream of liquid shot from my mouth onto the carpet. It had an acrid, rancid taste, like rotten orange juice.

I rushed to the kitchen to wash my mouth with water. Turning, I noticed the clock for the first time. It was 1:00 in the afternoon! But which afternoon? Later I discovered I'd been drugged for over twenty-four hours.

WAYNE TRANSFORMED

The phone was ringing. It was one of my employers, Mr. Stein.

"Where were you?" he asked. "I've called you three or four times."

"Well, uh, I was *out*."

"We saw Wayne on Bourbon Street," he continued.

"God, was he a mess—fighting some guy. The police hauled him away. He looked as crazy as hell. Are *you* all right, Perry?"

"Yes, yes, I'm O. K." I hung up the phone.

Why didn't I die last night? I had taken enough Nembutal to kill two people. Something — someone — had stopped me from dying. My head whirled.

Picking up the phone, I dialed the police station. "Do you have a Wayne Littlefield there? Yes, yes. . . How much is his bond? One hundred? Yes, I'll be right down."

I pulled on a pair of jeans and a blouse, and rushed out. I knew Wayne couldn't come back to live with me, but I felt responsible for his condition. I would bail him out, but he would have to go to a hospital until the drugs had left his system. I would be firm on this point.

Wayne was quite calm as we walked out of the police station. Too calm. It worried me. He didn't even argue when I suggested he go into the institution for treatment.

We were on the twenty-one-mile bridge, the longest bridge in the world, surrounded by the beautiful waters of Lake Ponchatrain. I was driving. We would soon be at Mandeville, the State mental institution.

Out of the corner of my eye, I watched Wayne. He looked like a little puppy that someone had thrown out in the cold. He was shivering, his eyes staring ahead vacantly, the fight gone out of him.

Come to think of it, the fight was gone out of me, too. The last few months of my life had been a living hell.

I'll never forget Wayne's face when I left him there. He looked like a corpse by then, white and dead inside. I got in my gold Chrysler New Yorker and drove away, tears streaming down my face. He hadn't even said, "Good bye." He couldn't talk. His mind had been burned too much by drugs.

It was three days later that my phone rang. It was Wayne. I could hardly believe his voice could sound so strong and firm only three days after being unable to speak!

"Perry! Perry!" he fairly shouted over the phone. "Something's happened! You've got to get back here right away. I have to talk to you—today!"

His voice sounded so strange, so excited. It didn't seem like him at all. I sped down the highway toward Mandeville.

As I parked the car, I saw Wayne sitting under a tree. He got up and started walking toward me. I could hardly believe my eyes. He was smiling! He looked absolutely radiant. It was almost as though someone had turned a light bulb on inside of him. He was literally glowing!

He hugged me, and pulled me toward the chairs under the tree, talking excitedly. "Perry, wait 'til you hear what happened to me last night!"

He was brimming with joy like a little child. What he said next was the most shocking thing I have ever heard in my life.

"Perry, I'm saved! I'm saved! I've got Jesus in my heart. I feel so good! It's wonderful!"

He was dancing with excitement.

"Oh, no," I thought. "He's *really* flipped out, just like Daddy."

"I know what you're thinking," he continued, "but I'm not crazy. I'm thinking straight for the first time in my life. It's true, Perry, it's true...Jesus is real! He loves me! He loves you! Perry, I've turned my life over to Him!"

For all that is in the world, the lust of the flesh, and the lust of the eyes, and the pride of life, is not of the Father, but is of the world.

1 John 2:16

Perry viewing Parade at Disneyworld 1973

For he that soweth to his flesh shall reap corruption!
Galations 6:8

Perry On Top of the Empire State Building After Surgery - 1972

Then I looked on all the works that my hands had wrought, and on the labour that I had laboured to do and behold all was vanity and vexation of spirit, and there was no profit under the sun.

Ecclesiastes 2:11

Perry in The Age of Aquarius two weeks before Salvation - Jan. 1974

9

Out of the Closet, Into the Kingdom

Driving back across the twenty-one mile bridge, my thoughts were filled with the things Wayne had said. But I was reacting to them in anger. I thought, "It's not rational. Who ever heard of a sane person turning their life over to a man who died two thousand years ago? Wayne's mind is warped. They're all nuts, all those damned Jesus Freaks—a bunch of reformed crooks and drug addicts!"

"Jesus! Jesus! Jesus!" That's all I'd heard from the bunch of rag-tag Jesus Freaks who passed out literature, and sang on Bourbon Street, telling everyone to "Repent." A couple of times they'd had the nerve to tell me I was "an abomination!"— whatever *that* meant. I was certain it wasn't good. They had even come into my shop several times and had told me everything we did there was from the devil! Who did they think they were anyway? They were only a bunch of whores, pimps, drug addicts, and numbskulls who couldn't make it in life without tripping out on religion! What right did they have to tell me I was wrong? They were *no* better than me—just a bunch of drop-outs trying to cram religion down somebody's throat!

Didn't they know that people came to Bourbon Street to have a good time, not to hear a sermon? They could go to church on Sunday if they wanted that. Besides, religion is a *personal* thing, nobody's business but your own! Couldn't they see that all the printed junk they passed out wound up on the street with people walking on it?

But the Jesus Freaks really frightened me, deep down inside. I couldn't understand why they always seemed so happy, were always smiling, even though they didn't take drugs! They seemed like the most abnormal, wild-eyed bunch of people I'd ever seen. Now Wayne was becoming one, too!

I phoned Wayne's psychiatrist as soon as I got in the house. "Doctor, Wayne says he has *Jesus* in his heart and that he's born again. What does all that mean?"

The doctor answered in carefully chosen, antiseptic words, "Miss Desmond, this is nothing to be overly concerned about. It happens quite often in mental institutions. Patients get so far down that they reach up and cling to this 'Jesus' as a sort of crutch. Do you understand?"

"Will Wayne be all right?"

"Oh, yes. I'm sure he'll get over it. He'll be all right in no time. In fact, those who have this type of experience seem to get well faster than others."

Wayne wrote to me every day. When I opened his letters, they were filled with verses from the Bible. The first one was an apology. I wondered what he had to apologize for; he hadn't done anything wrong, really. Then he sent me a letter that was almost nothing but a chapter from the Bible. It read:

Dear Perry,

I'm sorry for the way I acted the other day. I just wanted you to know that I love you and Jesus loves you, and He has a wonderful plan for your life. Just listen to this:

"Love is very patient and kind, never jealous or envious, never boastful or proud, never haughty or selfish or rude. Love does not demand its own way. It is not irritable or touchy. It does not hold grudges and will hardly even notice when others do it wrong...All the special gifts and powers from God will someday come to an end, but love goes on forever...faith, hope, and love—and the greatest of these is love"

(1 Corinthians 13:4-13 LB).

I'll call you at noon Thursday.

Love,

Wayne

It didn't sound like Wayne. In all the years I'd known him, I had received hundreds of letters from him, but he never wrote anything like that.

I decided that going back to work would be the best thing for me now. When Wayne phoned that Thursday, I was busy in The Age of Aquarius.

"How are you?" I asked.

"I'm feeling great. In fact, the doctor says I can get out next week."

"Oh, Wayne, that's beautiful. I'm excited! Maybe having a religious husband won't be so bad after all," I joked.

"Perry, that's what I called about. I can't come back to you any more. I'm going to a half-way house across from the church I'll be going to in Kenner. It's not that I don't love you, Perry. It's just that I've decided to dedicate my whole life to Jesus, and, after all, what we were doing was sin."

"Sin!" I screamed, "What do you mean, sin? Listen, you self-righteous Jesus Freak, if it's a sin to love you, then I'm a sinner. Go ahead, become a religious fanatic like Billy Graham, see if I care!"

I slammed the phone down in his ear.

BACK IN CIRCULATION

"I heard about Wayne," smirked the queen on the stool next

to me. "But you certainly don't look like you're in mourning."

"Well, I'm wearing black," I grinned, throwing back my shoulders to expose even more of my silicone bust above the thin, low-cut lace of my black dress.

I looked at myself in the mirror behind the bar. I looked good. In fact, I was stunning. I'd made a complete recovery to health in the past few weeks. I felt as good as new. And it felt good to be back in circulation. I chuckled at the thought of what "Holy Wayne" would think if he could see me now. He'd probably call me a real-life Jezebel!

The queen behind the bar brought me a drink. "Perry," he said, "this is from the boy at the other end of the bar. He wants to know if he can come and sit with you."

"Tell him yes," I smiled.

The boy and I had been eyeing each other for the past thirty minutes. He bore a striking resemblance to Errol Flynn when he was young; he was a real "ten star beauty," which was my way of describing a beautiful man.

"What's a nice girl like you doing in a place like this?" he said with smooth assurance, as he came and sat next to me.

"Where would you expect me to be, in church?" I joked, thinking again of Wayne.

His name was Craig, and he was twenty-one. He was a dope runner on his way to Texas to pick up a load of marijuana to sell in New York and New Jersey. When he told me that, I said, "Wow! That's the *last* thing I'd have suspected you'd be doing!"

"That's the idea," he grinned. "The police don't suspect me either."

He flipped out his fake IDs, showing that he was a student at Texas Tech. He told me that this was his fourth run, and he hadn't been stopped yet. "The big boss in New York says I'm their best runner," he bragged. "I'm only going to be here tonight. Let's don't waste it here. Let's go to your place."

I wanted to say "yes," but it dawned on me that Craig thought I was a woman.

"Let's have another drink," I said nervously. Then I blurted it out, "Craig, would you want to go with me if I were a man?"

"A what?" he laughed.

"A man."

"Baby, I'd go to bed with you if you were a kangaroo!" That was the beginning of our relationship.

Craig and I moved into a luxury apartment with a swimming pool right outside the door. I took him with me everywhere. I was *so* proud of him!

Once I overheard a lady say, "Isn't that woman's son nice looking." It went through me like a knife, but I tried to ignore it. She was right, though. I was getting older. But the boys I went with were the same age as before. Something was wrong, but I couldn't quite put my finger on it.

I took Craig to an expensive salon and bought him a wardrobe of expensive clothes. I bought him a 442 Oldsmobile Cutlass for his birthday.

Wayne came to visit us nearly every Sunday. Craig didn't like his "preaching," so we moved. But Wayne kept coming. I had slipped him our new address because I still wanted to see him. Craig and I began to fight. He was jealous of Wayne, even though he didn't need to be. Wayne and I were as innocent as two children by this time.

Wayne was trying every way he could think of to show me how to experience God as he had. He told me about Jesus over and over. He mailed Christian literature to me nearly *every* day. I didn't read any of it, but threw it all in a locker. I still have some of it.

One day Craig found a copy of the *Last News*, a Christian paper, printed like the daily news, that featured prophetic articles on the Second Coming of Christ.

"Perry, listen to this," Craig said, holding up the paper. "The dead come out of their graves! Bodies rise!" He laughed. "Can you imagine that!" We lay there on the bed laughing. "I see the fanatic has been sending you more of that religious garbage!" He took another puff of marijuana. We howled with laughter.

"Look out, Perry, the Anti-christ will get you!" He laughed and blew a smoke ring. But I wasn't really laughing inside. Somehow, deep in the pit of my stomach, I was beginning to feel that there was something a little sick about laughing at the Bible.

Wayne would phone me at work in the evenings, to tell me about Jesus. He kept coming on Sundays, after he went to church. Craig still didn't like it, so we started traveling more and more on weekends, to avoid Wayne's sermonizing.

But I liked having Wayne come—because I needed him emotionally. Craig and I were fighting so much now. I felt as if my mind was coming apart. I started flying Craig home to see his folks in New Jersey on weekends. Then I would drive to the half-way house to see Wayne. We'd go out to eat. He would tell me about Jesus. It usually ended with me crying.

One Sunday, while Craig was away, I cooked a big meal, a roast with all the trimmings. I could hardly wait for Wayne to come. By now I was eager to hear more from the Bible. I had never really read it, only the parts about baby Jesus in the manger and dead Jesus on the Cross. The Jesus Wayne read to me about was new. He was alive. He was dying for me, and rising again to give me hope. Wayne always told me He was doing all these things for *me*. I had never heard that before.

One day Wayne read a beautiful passage about Christ to me:

We despised him and rejected him—a man of sorrows, acquainted with bitterest grief. We turned our backs on him and looked the other way when he went by. He was despised and we didn't care. Yet it was our grief he bore, our sorrows that weighed him down. And we thought his troubles were a punishment from God, for his own sins! But he was wounded and bruised for our sins. He was chastised that we might have peace; he was lashed—and we were healed! We are the ones who strayed away like sheep! We, who left God's paths to follow our own. Yet God laid on him the guilt and sins of every one of us. He was oppressed and he was afflicted, yet he never said a word. He was brought as a lamb to the slaughter; and as a sheep before her shearers is dumb, so he stood silent before the ones condemning him. From prison and trial they led him away to his death. But who among the people of that day realized it was their sins that he was dying for—that he was suffering their punishment? He was buried like a criminal in a rich man's grave; but he had done no wrong, and had never spoken an evil word. Yet it was the Lord's good plan to bruise him and fill him with grief. But when his soul has been made an offering for sin, then he shall have a multitude of children, many heirs. He shall live again and God's program shall prosper in his hands...he bore the sins of many, and he pled with God for sinners   (Isaiah 53:1-12 LB).

Wayne turned to me when he had finished reading. "Perry, Jesus died for you. How much more could anyone love you?"

This went on for over a year, until the situation between Craig and I deteriorated beyond any possible hope of repair. One night Craig came to me and said, "Perry, I need a real woman." Then he was gone...for several nights.

When he came back he had a sixteen-year-old girl on his arm. She was very unattractive, skinny, with stringy blond hair. But she was a real woman.

"Perry, I want a real woman." How often I had heard those words over the years.

Dresses only covered my masculinity.

Makeup only masked it.

Silicone only reshaped it.

Surgery only mutilated it.

Underneath, in every cell of my body, the truth was recorded ten million times, in every gene.

I was a man!

No matter what I did, where I went, what I said, how much money I spent, or how often I was operated on—*nothing* really changed. Every man I ever lived with always came to the point Craig had now reached, "Perry, I want a real woman." She might be boney, while I was voluptuous; she might be poor, while I was rich; she might be naive, while I knew every art of seduction—but she would be real—and I would always be false, no matter what I did.

"Perry, I need a real woman."

"I can't stand to hear that! I can't stand it! Not even one more time!"

Then, suddenly, I felt... happy. That's the only word I can think of to describe it. It was a strange, light feeling, like something was being released around me...within me.

Craig was, after all, only a body to me. And I'd had so many bodies that...well, he was just another one. I'd never thought of it that way before! A hush fell over my heart.

It was three in the morning when my sister phoned.

"Perry, Mother is very sick. She's in the hospital."

I sat bolt upright in bed. "What do you mean, very sick?" I demanded.

"Well, Perry, they don't expect her to live."

My heart sank. She promised to call me back the next day to give me a further report.

I knew why Mother was so sick. She had been working too hard, and she had to take care of her brother as well. It was just too much for her. A wave of sadness swept over me because of all the mean things I had done to her—the arguments, the embarrassments, the scenes. I took some sleeping pills and cried for a while before drifting off into a troubled sleep.

The next day my sister phoned as she had promised.

Mother had diabetes, high blood pressure, and an enlarged heart. The doctor said she'd probably make it, but she would have to take better care of herself.

My sister broke into tears telling me all this. "Perry," she said, "Mother looks so bad and I'm afraid."

I comforted her as best I could, hung up, and dialed the hospital. They put the phone to Mother's ear. When she spoke, she sounded very far away. "Perry...is that you?" It seemed like she was speaking through a long tunnel.

"Yes, Mother, it's me! Mother, Mother...I love you!"

"I'm glad to hear you, Perry, but I'm so tired..." Her voice trailed off.

"Mother, I'm coming to see you. I'm leaving right away."

There was a long silence on her end of the line. Then she spoke. This time her voice was very precise and clear. "No, Perry, I'd rather remember you as you were..."

There was a clicking sound on the line, like the receiver had fallen from her hand onto the floor. Then I heard a dial tone. The phone was dead.

"No, Perry, I'd rather remember you as you *were*..." I was crushed. Mother, too, was unwilling to accept me as a woman. She didn't even want me in her dying moments.

I turned to the only person I had in the world—Wayne.

It was so good to hear his voice on the other end of the line. "Wayne," I cried, "Mother's dying, and she doesn't even want to see me. I need your help...I'm all alone."

"Perry, we're having a meeting at my church at 7:30 tonight. I want you to come. It will do you good."

"O. K., Wayne, I'll go," I heard myself saying.

I could hear them singing as I approached the church building:

> Would you be free from the burden of sin?
>   There's power in the blood, power in the blood;
> Would you o'er evil a victory win?
>   There's wonderful power in the blood.
>
> Would you be free from your passion and pride?
>   There's power in the blood, power in the blood;
> Come for a cleansing to Calvary's tide;
>   There's wonderful power in the blood.

I looked through the window. They were all standing and clapping along with the piano music. Their faces looked so happy. But I had nothing to be happy about. What was I doing there? Why had I let Wayne talk me into this? The song continued:

> Would you be whiter, much whiter than snow?
>   There's power in the blood, power in the blood;
> Sin stains are lost in its life-giving flow;
>   There's wonderful power in the blood.

I turned to walk away. This certainly wasn't for me.

"Perry!" It was Wayne's voice. I turned. He came to me. "Let's go in, Perry." I was too weak to resist him. I followed him up the stairs. They were still singing the chorus of the hymn:

> There is power, power, Wonder working power
> In the blood of the Lamb;
> There is power, power, Wonder working power
> In the precious blood of the Lamb.

I stopped short in the hall. "Wayne, I can't go in there with all those people. I. . . I'm a Catholic. Those people are so emotional. . .I just came here to see you. I don't want to go in there. . . please?"

Just then the door opened and a chubby-faced lady in a long dress came out. She reached out her hand for mine. "Hi there," she smiled. "Are you a friend of Wayne's?"

He spoke up. "Yes, yes she is."

"Well, don't stand out *here*; come on in," she said, steering us into the auditorium.

Wayne took my hand and led me down the aisle of the church. I looked like a puzzle with the main piece missing. My clothes were pretty messy and my makeup was smeared from crying. But the people kept smiling at me.

A woman had come from the audience to speak at the

front of the church. She opened her Bible and began:

I would like to talk about the flesh. The Bible says, "If you sow to the flesh, of the flesh you will reap corruption." You know, brothers and sisters, our flesh is undependable. What it wants today, it doesn't want tomorrow. One minute it's hot and the next, it's cold. It's never the same. And it's never satisfied. You just can't please it. Brothers and sisters, we need to die to the flesh and live in the Spirit.

"What is she talking about?" I thought. What kind of a place did Wayne bring me to, anyway? I looked around at the people. They looked so different from those I knew on Bourbon Street, almost as though they had come from another time or place.

None of the women had on any makeup. Their hair was long and uncut; their dresses were long too, down to the floor. It was the same with the little girls.

The men all had "white sidewall" haircuts, short over the ears, and white shirts with ties. It looked strange to me, but I felt something I had never experienced in my life. It was Christian love. These people really loved each other. I could *feel* it.

Stranger still, I could feel their love for me. They all smiled at me—with such warmth. I felt something new and unexplainable... a kind of non-sensual warmth and tenderness. It filled the room.

Then the man in the pulpit pointed at me.

"Who is that?" I whispered to Wayne.

"He's our pastor."

"You there!" The man with the pointing finger was talking to me in a kindly but commanding voice. "You there, you're not saved, are you?"

I shook my head no.

"Come on up to the altar and kneel down. We're going to pray for you to know Jesus."

"Is he crazy?" I thought. ME GO UP THERE. . . and kneel in front of all these people? I wouldn't do that for him or anybody, including Jesus Christ. I got up and started to leave the room.

His voice shot through me like an arrow. "You can't run from God! When you get home, God's going to be there. We're going to claim your soul for the Kingdom of Heaven. Get up, brothers and sisters. Let's pray for this woman to get saved."

I could hear the congregation rise to their feet as I beat a retreat for the door. Then they were praying, all at once. The babble reached my ears even as the engine turned over and my car pulled onto the street.

"Whew, I'm glad I got out of that!" I said out loud to myself as I sped toward the French Quarter.

When I got home, I locked the windows and doors, crawled

into bed, and waited for God. I kept remembering what the minister said, "When you get home, God will be there." But God didn't show up, and I soon went to sleep.

"Why didn't I go up to that altar?" I thought as I lay in bed the next morning. "I really do want what Wayne has. I should have gone up there for prayer. It was my stupid pride that kept me from doing it. I'll bet pride has stopped a lot of people from getting saved."

I got dressed and went down to The Age of Aquarius. It seemed so drab and lifeless now. The place had run down terribly in the last few weeks. I was losing interest in everything—even money. And *that* worried me.

I was the first one to get there. I went in and looked around the room. It seemed so strange—the obscene T-shirts, the head shop, the Egyptian Reading Room—the place even smelled bad. I made up my mind right then and there to close the Egyptian Reading Room like Wayne had suggested. I told the astonished "readers" when they arrived for work.

Going back to my house, I decided to read all the Christian literature Wayne had given me over the months. I dug it out and spent the day poring over it.

It was Wednesday night. There was a Baptist church right next to the laundromat I used. I remembered the sign, "Prayer Meeting—Wednesday, 7:30 P. M." At the bottom of the sign it said, "Jesus Loves You!"

I went by The Age of Aquarius and asked one of the boys to go with me. We were a little late getting there. We sat at the back. A man was reading the Bible from behind the pulpit. Then he began to speak:

You can't make a deal with God. You've got nothing to deal with. Once the Gospel hook is set and God begins to reel you in, you can fight all you want, but soon you'll tire out, and God will swoop you up in His net of love.

I began to cry.

When the service was ended, I walked up to the minister at the front. "I want Jesus. I want to be saved," I said through my tears.

An old deacon came over and pulled the minister away from me. He whispered something in the minister's ear. I didn't like the way he was glancing at me while he spoke. It didn't seem like he wanted me to get saved. I discovered later that he knew who I was and was afraid if I got saved there I'd join his church.

The minister came back to me. He told me his name was Dr. Humphries. I told him my story briefly. A look of amazement spread over his face. He assured me he would be at my house Saturday afternoon.

I left the church feeling better, but still unsaved.

When Saturday came, I was ready. I paced the floor, waiting for Dr. Humphries to arrive. Then the bell rang. I jumped. It was him. I showed him in and we sat down. He opened his Bible and showed me five verses from the book of Romans, explaining each one as I read them.

As it is written, There is none righteous, no, not one

Romans 3:10

For all have sinned, and come short of the glory of God

Romans 3:23

For the wages of sin is death

Romans 6:23

"Now, Perry, that verse shows us what will happen to you if you continue to break God's Laws and live in sin. You will perish. See what it says," he pointed his finger at the verse. "The wages, the pay-off, of sin is death. That death means eternal separation from God. That's what will happen to you if you continue in sin."

But God commendeth his love toward us, in that,
while we were yet sinners Christ died for us

Romans 5:8

"Perry, we are all sinners. All of us, from all walks of life, have broken God's Commands. The rich and the poor, the straights and the gays, the moralist and the swinger, all of us are guilty. That is why Romans 5:8 tells us that Christ died for us while we were still sinners. We needed to have Him die in our place to pay for our sins. If we don't accept His death as a payment for our sins, we will have to pay for them ourselves. He went to hell on the Cross. If you turn from your sins and ask Him to forgive you, His death on the Cross will take the place of the punishment you deserve. He paid the penalty for your sins. But you must repent, turn from sin, and trust Him as your Saviour."

For whosoever shall call upon the name of the
Lord shall be saved

Romans 10:13

"Perry, will you call on Jesus to forgive and save you? Will you do it now?"

He had hardly finished speaking when I started crying. "Can I get saved now?"

"Yes, Perry, let's get down on our knees."

We did.

"Now, Perry, repeat the following prayer after me:

Jesus, come into my heart, forgive my sins, wash me in your blood...

When I said those words, I felt something clawing inside of me. It ripped out with a horrible sensation. We finished the prayer. I ran to my room, threw myself on my knees by the side of my bed.

Dr. Humphries followed me in. "What are you doing?" he asked softly,

"I'm telling Jesus my sins."

"He knows them," he replied,

"I just want to make sure," I said through my tears.

"That's good, take all the time confessing you need. And, Perry, you need the warmth and fellowship of a Bible-believing church to grow in Christ."

He left quietly and I was alone, confessing my sins to the living God.

I don't know how long I stayed there on my knees, but when I got up, I felt like someone had scrubbed me from the inside. I felt clean and pure, for the first time in my life.

Jesus had set me free!

10

A Eunuch
for the Lord

... neither let the eunuch say, Behold, I am a dry
tree. For thus saith the Lord unto the eunuchs
that . . . choose the things that please me, and
take hold of my covenant; Even unto them will I
give in mine house and within my walls a place
and a name better than of sons and of daughters;
I will give them an everlasting name, that shall
not be cut off.

Isaiah 56:3-5 KJV

The blessings God promises to eunuchs in Isaiah 56 have
become a reality to me since I received Jesus Christ into my life
that afternoon in February, 1974.

Slowly God has been molding me, making me over into the kind of person He wants me to be. I'm not sure yet what the end product will be, but I'm on the way. As someone has said, "Be patient—God isn't through with me yet!"

It amazes me what has happened during the past four years, as the Lord has led me along on this journey toward heaven. Each year I have seen His name on my life.

1974

In February I became a Christian. It was such a thrill knowing that my sins were forgiven. I loved the Bible. I loved to pray. I was in church every time the door opened. I literally read the Bible night and day.

After I had been at church for about two months, I got into a Bible class. The teacher was good. I trusted his judgment. One day I asked him if I had to start dressing like a man again.

He came to my apartment in Bourbon Street that night. We sat on the steps in the lamplight. He showed me Deuteronomy 22:5:

The woman shall not wear that which pertaineth unto a man, neither shall a man put on a woman's garment; for all that do so are abomination unto the Lord thy God.

He looked at me and said, "Perry, no matter what you have

done, no matter what the doctors have added or taken away, you're still a man; God created you as a man. That is what you are, and that is what you must dress as."

Then it hit me like a thunderbolt — how I had been living a lie. Now God wanted me to live the truth. It would require a complete change.

At first I thought I could never do it.

"How can I EVER go back to dressing like a man?" I asked.

"Let's go inside and pray about it," the Bible teacher said calmly. We did, and a great peace came over me. The next day I bought men's clothing — for the first time in six years!

Buying the clothes wasn't easy. Everyone in the clothing store was staring at me, wondering why this "woman" was buying men's clothes. I grabbed a shirt and pants and headed for the dressing room.

Emerging rather sheepishly, I made my way to the mirror on the other side of the room. I looked. It was ironic — I was like a lesbian in men's clothing — the same way I had looked at Daddy's funeral six years earlier.

Soon I was used to my new attire, however, and the great adventure of ministering for Jesus began.

I started to work for Christ by buying thousands of Christian tracts and passing them out on Bourbon Street. I didn't win many folks to Christ, but I made some good

Christian friends. Soon they were urging me to turn The Age of Aquarius into a Christian mission.

In April of 1974 I did just that. The Age of Aquarius became The Good News Church. We cleaned out the occult junk and put in Christian literature. We set up a referral center for those with problems too deep for us to handle. It was great having church services where I had once worshiped at the altar of lust.

Wayne got married in August. I was the best man. I wonder how many times that's happened in history—a former lover of the groom acting as best man?

1975

I was now getting many invitations to speak. News of my conversion was spreading. People were eager to hear the whole story. I began traveling to different churches for speaking engagements.

We taped a TV special titled, "Look What They Did To Bourbon Street." It aired on Easter Sunday morning in New Orleans and in the afternoon, by cable, throughout the South. The response was fantastic. People were writing to me for weeks.

Then I was offered the chance to do a daily radio program. It was a talk show with interviews. We had a good audience and the show became quite popular.

1976

When the Mardi Gras came to New Orleans, we were ready for it! Various Christian ministries from the area got together to proclaim "Jesus is Lord of Mardi Gras." In the midst of all the revelry of this yearly debauchery, we won hundreds of people to Christ. It was a great way to start the year!

I went to Orlando, Florida for "Jesus '76." This was a gathering of Christians from across the nation. Many great speakers were there with the top musical groups of the Christian world. A huge tent held booths filled with Christian books. It was thrilling. I had a small booth where I gave away our "Good News Church" literature. I had printed a booklet on my life story which we sold.

In June I went to Melodyland, the famed church near Disneyland, in California. They held the first congress of ministries to former homosexuals there. It was called the Exodus conference, "Exodus" standing for our *coming out* of the bondage of sexual sin into the promised land of faith in Christ.

It was a wonderful conference. I met Jim Kasper and Mike Bussee, the two men who run the gay ministry at Melodyland. I also met Kent Philpott and Frank Worthen, the directors of "Love in Action," the ministry to former homosexuals which is based in San Francisco. Kent had just published his book on homosexuality, *The Third Sex?* (Logos Books, 1976).

1977

Anita Bryant came to sing at the New Orleans Summer Pops. It was only a few days after the vote in Dade County, Florida, when the gays were voted down on the homosexual equal rights bill there.

The entire homosexual community of New Orleans was up in arms. We Christians decided to form Christians Behind Anita, a coalition of Christian groups who supported the singer.

On the night she performed, we had a Rally for Righteousness in front of the auditorium where she was singing.

Then I enrolled at Christ for the Nations in Dallas, Texas, where I grew in the Lord and studied His word. During this time I spoke in many different prisons with Chaplain Ray and Cookie Rodrequiz.

1978

After a year in Dallas, God began speaking to me about starting a ministry in St. Louis. I had been there many times and spoken in many churches, but I was always grieved, because there was no on-going ministry to the Gay community.

I prayed, and God spoke to me to join forces with a dynamic group, and I enrolled in a Bible College at New Life Evangelistic Center in St. Louis. I also served there as Co-Director with Gina Evans (a former lesbian) for a new ministry called C. O. A. L. (Come Out and Live).

I believe in these last days that God is going to pick out certain cities to show the world His glory. I believe St. Louis is one of these cities.

I have been saved for almost five years now, and I can't believe how much Jesus has changed my life. Sometimes, when I look into the mirror, I have to pinch myself to make sure I'm not just dreaming. I don't know what the future holds for me, but I do know Who holds the future . . . His name is Jesus, and He's everything to me . . .

Perry's written journal ended at this point. However, for six years until his death in June of 1984 he continued to commute between his ministry efforts in California and his friends and budding efforts in Missouri. He spent a lot of time with Harry Douma and the people of Camp Penuel and with his friends in the St. Louis area. He especially enjoyed attending the annual Christian Booksellers Association conventions, where he was often seen with a celebrity in tow dragging him or her to meet people or to have a picture taken. He was pure energy and exuded love and compassion wherever he went.

The last time we saw Perry he was very excited and enthusiastic about a movie of his life, which a Christian motion picture group had signed to produce. He introduced the us to the young actor who was to play him in the movie version of his life — a cute freckled-faced, redheaded boy.

A TRIBUTE: PERRY'S TRANSFORMATION

Perry's transformation was truly miraculous — a metamorphosis into a life full of light and purpose. From a life of dependency on drugs and alcohol to freedom from addiction, and an infilling of peace. His story confirms many similar stories of lives lost to despair and hopelessness suddenly changed to lives full of the love and the presence of Jesus.

There are those in the world, and even those in the church, who may reject you, but Jesus Christ will not. He has been waiting your entire life for the chance to meet you.

Perhaps Perry's story leads you to a completely new revelation for your life —that God loves you. We hope that you see this. This love for you is, in fact, the reason God gave us the Bible, from Genesis to its end. It is summed up in 1 John 4:16…

"God is love."

Paul furthers this thought when he prays that we might come to know the love of Jesus, a love that is so great that it is "beyond our human understanding" (Eph. 3:19). And in the

Book of Romans, Paul describes the love of Jesus as being more powerful than death or life, past or present, angels or demons, or anything else in all of creation!

Furthermore, Jesus invites you to come to know Him personally, for He is neither arrogant nor rude, but rather gentle and humble:

> "Come to Me all who are weary and heavy laden, and I will give you rest. For I am gentle and humble in spirit."
>
> Matt 11:28–29

Now is your chance to surrender to Him your wounds, your pain and your hopelessness, your regrets, and He will meet you now, in your time of need. Jesus is always faithful, His love will never fail, and He will never leave you or forsake you.

You should know that as you pray the salvation prayer that Perry lists in the following pages, you will become an entirely new creation. This may seem hard to fathom, but you are washed as white as snow, and become a newborn child in the kingdom of God. Some of your wounds may be deep and they may take time to work their way out — we recommend prayer with a community of fellow believers who practice deliverance, and to pursue an empowerment known as the Baptism in the

Holy Spirit.

This is the good news of God's love, but it is just the beginning of an incredible journey of miracles, walking daily with the Son of God. We have seen literally thousands of healings come through prayer, including blind eyes opening, deaf ears being healed, the lame walking, and the terminally ill set free from their disease. There is simply no limit to the power, or love, of God. He promises to take the worst that our enemy, Satan, throws at us and to turn it around for our own good as we submit our cause to Him.

Below, you will learn of one more life transformed by the love of Jesus Christ. A man dying from the advanced stages of AIDS, with no hope, in the pit of despair, until he met the love and the healing power of Jesus Christ...

BRET: DYING OF AIDS, WITH TWO WEEKS LEFT TO LIVE

When we found Bret in early 1998, he was in a coma, hooked up to a life support system, in the ICU ward of a local hospital. We were told by the doctors that he had only two weeks left to live. He was dying from the advanced stages of AIDS. There was no hope for him, and even his family and friends had decided his life was over.

When a friend, Ruth, told us about his condition, she also told us how compelled she was in her heart to pray for his healing. That, clearly, was a tall order of faith, but her excitement about the power of God encouraged us to tackle Bret's needs through prayer and fasting. So we decided to set aside one day a week to pray and fast for Bret (there were only three of us at the time in a small and very humble prayer group). Each time we would fast, we would gather at night and pray for his life, his health and his future with the Lord.

I must admit that my faith was not that great. Each time we would meet, my first question was not "is he healed?" but rather "is he still alive?" Fortunately for us, Jesus tells us that even with faith the size of a mustard seed, great things can happen. Bret's case was no exception. At the end of the four weeks, Ruth informed us that he had come out of his coma and was stabilized enough to move out of the ICU ward and into a regular hospital room.

Then, after coming out of his coma, they transferred him from the hospital to an AIDS hospice to die.

By then, he had dropped from 220 lbs. to only 120 lbs, and was so weak he could barely speak out the request for Ruth to "keep praying!"

Ruth visited him often in the AIDS hospice, continuing to stress to him the power of God, and how Jesus is still in the business of healing people. Despite being surrounded by death on a daily basis, within a matter of a few months he was discharged from the hospice.

Astonished, we called Bret to learn of the events surrounding his departure. He told us the following:

> "When I moved from the ICU ward to the AIDS hospice, the doctors were always doing tests, one blood test after the other. Finally, after months of blood work at the hospice, they told me the most wonderful news: they could no longer find any evidence of AIDS in my blood stream! So they released me. They even told me that they could no longer find the HIV that caused the AIDS in the first place!"

Bret was healed almost twenty years ago and is today working with an AIDS Hospice program. We rejoice in Bret's healing, and are awed by the love and mercy of Bret's Healer, Jesus Christ.

Perry
Answers Questions:

"QUESTIONS I AM MOST FREQUENTLY ASKED..."

1. What is the difference between a transsexual and a transvestite?

   A transsexual believes that they are members of the opposite sex, and are willing to undergo sex-change surgery to become physically the sex they identify with. A transvestite only likes to cross-dress in clothes of the opposite sex, but in no way wants to become a member of the opposite sex.

2. Is a man who has a sex-change really a woman afterwards?

   It took me a long time to realize that God doesn't make mistakes. If he makes you a man, that's what you are—no matter what doctors add or take away! In Jesus there is no identity crisis. He restores our true sexual identity.

3. What should a person do if they discover that a son or daughter is a transsexual?

   First of all, don't stop loving them, and don't alienate them by condemning them. You must realize that they are not doing this just for the fun of it. They are

171

very serious. The doctors say that they must change the body to fit the mind. I say that the mind of Jesus Christ must take over your mind, then you won't need to change the body at all. The answer to the transsexual's problem is to be born again and to learn to accept themselves as God made them, not as they believe they should be.

4. What do you think about the Christians who were unkind to you before you received Christ?

At first I was shocked. But after much prayer, I realized that there are both good and bad Christians, and that I shouldn't condemn the bad ones. If I did that, I would be just as bad as they are. The Bible says that we should manifest the love of Jesus to the lost, no matter what sin they are practicing. We should hate the sin, but love the sinner. That is what Jesus did. I have forgiven everyone who was unkind to me—just as God has forgiven me.

5. Do you believe homosexuals and transsexuals are demon possessed?

I do not believe all homosexuals and transsexuals are demon possessed any more than I believe all unsaved heterosexuals are demonized. I do believe that demons are real, though. [Anyone interested in the subject of demonization and deliverance might like to read a book on this subject, *Power for Deliverance: Songs of Deliverance.* Additionally, you can find information on deliverance in a book entitled *Pigs in the Parlor.*]

6. What can churches do to help homosexuals and transsexuals?

Today, many churches have ministries and hotlines to the gay community. I think this is healthy. The Bible-believing churches must reach out to those with sexual sins, just as they must reach out to those with other sins.

7. Do all homosexuals and transsexuals have to become celibates like you to be Christians?

No. As more and more gay people are getting saved, we are discovering that when persons turn their sexuality over to Jesus Christ, they begin to grow into normal human beings, as God created them to be. I know many personally who are now happily married. Others, like myself, become perfectly happy and fulfilled in the celibate life style, although I never thought this possible before my conversion.

8. Can you practice homosexuality and still be a Christian?

No. I have read most of the literature distributed by the gay churches and organizations, and I remain totally unconvinced that the Bible condones homosexuality. The practice of homosexuality is not compatible with Biblical Christianity. I suggest that Romans 1:26-27; 1 Corinthians 6:9-11; and Galatians 5:19-21 be read by those who have questions in this area. The gymnastics of those who reinterpret these verses leave me unconvinced.

9. **How can the Holy Spirit help homosexuals and transsexuals?**

> Life in the Spirit is the answer. When I was filled with the Holy Spirit, real power for service flooded me. Now I can lead a victorious life for Christ and witness of His love with power. I had to give up the sins in my life and ask Him to fill me with His Spirit in a definite experience.

10. **How does one become a "born again" Christian?**

> By repenting of sin and receiving Jesus Christ. The Bible says that you have sinned (Romans 3:23). It also says that "God commendeth his love toward us, in that while we were yet sinners, Christ died for us" (Romans 5:8). Now you must call on the Lord, and ask Him to forgive you (Romans 10:13). When you are ready to do that, pray this prayer:

Dear Lord Jesus,

I know that I am a sinner and need your forgiveness. I believe that you died for my sins. I turn from my sins now and invite you to come into my heart and life. I will trust you as Savior and follow you as Lord, and live in the fellowship of your church. Amen.

From the Man who Introduced Perry to Jesus Christ

It was a Wednesday in February of 1974. I was teaching a Bible study to a small group of people at the Vieux Carre Baptist Church in the French Quarter of New Orleans.

A couple came in late for the service and sat behind the rest of the group. When the meeting was over, I spoke to the latecomers and asked if they had just come for a visit. The "lady" replied that they had come to be saved. The speaker, who gave every appearance of being a woman, was, in fact, Perry Desmond.

A few days after this meeting I again shared the good news of Christ with Perry. This time, at Perry's home, Perry asked Christ to become his Savior and Lord.

Then he took me to meet his friends at the shop he ran on Bourbon Street. He was very excited about being a Christian. I was somewhat shocked by the shop (it seemed to be mostly pornography). But the most astonished people of all were Perry's friends, who were stunned to hear that Perry Desmond had "gotten religion."

The reason for this amazement and the form it took are a part of the story of this book. But the important part of this story is the way in which Perry's enthusiastic testimony for Christ has validated the Christian faith for so many people. Perry Desmond is an extraordinary person whose life is a transparent witness to the grace of God .

Dr. Fischer Humphries
Professor of Theology
New Orleans Baptist Theological Seminary

Pat Boone and Perry Desmond

"Escape from homosexuality is a supernatural process. Return from transsexuality is a miracle! Perry Desmond has been there and back, and his story is electrifying."

- Pat Boone

Sid (Jody) Ford and Perry

Former friends reunite at the Mardi Gras in New Orleans. Jody was amazed at the change in Perry's life. Tragically, shortly after this picture, Sid returned to Birmingham where he was shot to death in a parking lot.

Perry, in the Years After He Dedicated His Life to Jesus

Perry with Chaplain Ray and wife Leola

Brother Harry Douma, Haralan Popov and Perry Desmond

Perry Desmond, Zola Levitt and Charles McPheeters

www.ingramcontent.com/pod-product-compliance
Lightning Source LLC
Chambersburg PA
CBHW060040150626
46553CB00017BA/601